HISTORY

MAYO

HISTORIC TALES OF
MAYO

EAMONN HENRY

I ndíl-chuimhne m'athair 'gus mo mháthair;
ar dheis Dé go raibh a n-anam.

In loving memory of my parents;
may they rest in peace.

First published 2018

The History Press Ireland
50 City Quay
Dublin 2
Ireland
www.thehistorypress.ie

© Eamonn Henry, 2018

The right of Eamonn Henry to be identified as the Author
of this work has been asserted in accordance with the
Copyright, Designs and Patents Act 1988.

British Library Cataloguing in Publication Data.
A catalogue record for this book is available from the British Library.

ISBN 978 0 7509 8692 2

Typesetting and origination by The History Press
Printed in Great Britain

CONTENTS

FOREWORD

This is a family affair! I ask you, dear reader, to hold that sentiment close as you go through the following pages of this anthology. Many of the events and customs of these tales will seem almost alien to many of the modern Irish. Famine ships, rebellions fought with pikes and cross-country cart rides seem like features of a modern fantasy series. But then mass evictions, emigration and Machiavellian landlords strike an immediate and familiar chord. These circumstances were the hard reality for the subjects of these *Historic Tales of Mayo*.

In 1979, my brother Eamonn compiled numerous stories, yarns and anecdotes that our late father, John Edward, had assembled. The initial publication was *Tales from the West of Ireland* – an immense moment for Eamonn and our father. For my father, it represented the culmination of a lifetime spent assimilating spoken tales and being an acclaimed storyteller himself (note there is a stark difference between a storyteller and someone who just talks!). In spite of his travels and the places he worked, he maintained a solid and unbreakable connection with his homelands: its people, its history, its identity.

For Eamonn, our siblings and I, growing up, the forthcoming passages were an everyday part of our lives. They were not merely folklore or 'dad's yarns' – they were accounts of people and places we knew and appreciated. Relatives, neighbours and town locals featured prominently. This proximity to the source material instilled a pride in us and aroused a curiosity that has lasted throughout the decades since we left Ballydrum. Few more than Eamonn can exemplify that connection (himself an already published author on the subject of Maigh Éo, the Land of the Shamrock and Heather).

And so when he asked me to scribe the Foreword for this book, I was both humbled and very proud. Sons and brothers continuing their father's passion. My own children, in whom we have nurtured a respect for 'the West', assisted me with this piece and supported Eamonn through the greater work where possible. So as we started so shall we finish – always remember that this is a family affair!

Michael Henry, 2018

PREFACE

The tales in this book are mainly based on the collection of folktales written by my late father, John Edward Henry, with some additions made by me. My father was a tireless collector of the lore and legends of former generations. The last six tales were written by me but they are based on conversations I had with my dad and also on his notes, which were passed on to me.

My father was born in Ballydrum, a village near Swinford, East Mayo, in 1904. His father, Patrick Martin, ran a busy brick-making operation, a business he had inherited from his own father before him. Many private houses and public buildings throughout East Mayo were part-built with bricks from Ballydrum and the house was a hive of activity during John Edward's early years. He developed a love of storytelling and, perhaps more importantly, of listening to the stories and tales of the older people who regularly stopped by.

In 1928, he emigrated to the US in 1926, where he spent a number of years working in Chicago before returning to take over the running of the family farm and to marry his childhood sweetheart, Margaret Salmon, from Curneen, Claremorris.

He spent a number of years working as a charge hand or 'ganger' for Mayo County Council, carrying out road maintenance, bridge-building and pier-maintenance projects. From conversations with local people, especially those of older generations, he gathered much of the material that would later form the basis of his collection.

He took a supply of pencils and wire-bound notebooks with him whenever his work took him away from home and he would pass long winter evenings making notes and annotations as he listened to the accounts of those with whom he chatted about former times. When he returned home at weekends, he used those notes to write up more complete accounts in longhand.

He was a prolific writer and his work appeared in many local magazines and community publications. A collection of his stories, *Tales from the West of Ireland*, was published by the Mercier Press in 1979 and was re-issued in 2000. He was also a regular contributor to an American travel company's newsletter, writing commentaries on Irish current affairs.

Some of the stories to be found in this book have appeared before in book form or in magazines and periodicals, but the majority have not been published before.

Before his death in 1986, my father passed his folklore collection of stories, songs, myths and legends on to me and expressed the hope that I would make them available for future generations. The tales in this book form part of his legacy.

Note: The reader should keep in mind that most of the tales in this book were composed in the period between 1976 and 1980; therefore, references to current events have to be qualified.

Eamonn Henry, 2018

1

THE YEAR OF
THE FRENCH

When the little French expeditionary force under General Humbert landed at Kilcummin, near Killala, North Mayo, on 22 August 1798, they were received with open arms by the local people, who looked on their coming as a wholehearted attempt by Napoleon to free Ireland from English domination. They would not have dreamed of regarding it as an operation to divert a sizeable amount of England's land and sea forces from theatres of war on the Continent.

The ensuing campaign, which resulted in the capture of Ballina and then Castlebar and the clearing of County Mayo of all enemy forces by the Franco-Irish force, was a brilliant opening to the short-lived insurrection in the west. The fatal delay of almost two weeks in Castlebar unfortunately gave the enemy time to regroup and plan counter-attacks and encircling movements unhindered.

During the French stay in the town, they were wined and dined in the most lavish way by the people of the town and the surrounding countryside. The victory of the Franco-Irish forces at Castlebar and the proclamation of the Republic of Connacht under President John Moore infused the people of Castlebar and the rest of the country with renewed spirit.

Those who did join for active service came loaded with gifts of meat, butter, poultry, eggs, fish, etc., for the troops. One party came with a steer that had been cooked in a quarry near the town on heated slabs of limestone, a custom dating back to Hannibal's time.

Gifts of clothing and footwear donated by merchants from Castlebar and the nearby towns also arrived. Drilling the raw recruits and getting them accustomed to the French muskets, swords and small arms took up valuable time. Despite all this, it has been stated that the Irish recruits who stuck to or reverted to their traditional weapon, the pike, gave a better account of themselves and inspired more fear among the Redcoats at Carricknagat and Ballinamuck, as well as in the capture of Castlebar.

A large contingent came from the Newport–Ballycroy area. A company from Ballycroy and Erris had previously marched to Ballina to join. A body of insurgents from Westport and Louisburgh included two Augustinian friars, Fr Myles Prendergast and Fr Michael Gannon. This force was led by Johnny Gibbons, locally nicknamed Johnny the Outlaw. From the Knock–Aughamore district came two strong companies under Captain Seamas O'Malley and Richard Jordan. A company of recruits came from Killedan and Bohola parishes under Henry Valentine Jordan of Rosslevin.

A large company from the glens around Nephin Mountain, who joined on the route from Ballina to Castlebar, was led by Captain Peadar Jordan of Coolnabinna. Jordan escaped to Achill Island after the collapse of the rising and died suddenly while on the run there. He composed the poem '*Cúl na Binn*', one of the finest poems of the '98 period.

It is worth mentioning that one of the martyred priests of the Penal Days in East Mayo was Fr Fulgentius Jordan, so the Jordans should hold an honoured place in the turbulent history of Mayo.

Another local leader who joined the Franco-Irish force just before the fight for Castlebar with a strong body of pikemen was Captain Willie Mangan of Sion Hill.

According to local tradition, the first rout of any of the Redcoat regiments guarding the approaches to the town took place at Sion Hill. This, coupled with a flanking attack from the west side of the town by around 300 pikemen, is believed to be the main factor in the complete rout of England's regular soldiers and the hated Irish militia. This event has gone down in Mayo's history as 'The Races of Castlebar'.

Four years previously, the people of Castlebar and the neighbourhood had flocked onto Main Street to watch two wine-soaked
rack-renting landlords fight, or attempt to fight, a sword duel. Caesar
French of Oughterard and the local bully boy, George Robert (or, as
he was nicknamed, 'Fighting') Fitzgerald of Turlough House, were
the contestants.

During the scuffle, Fitzgerald's spurs got entangled in his great-
coat and he fell to the ground. Immediately, French placed his foot
on Fitzgerald's chest and pointed his sword at his throat, with the
familiar duellist's demand that he surrender or die. Just then, the
crowd surged forward to save their local oppressor, with the result
that French was forced to flee for his life. He wisely had his attendant
waiting with two saddled horses at the top of the town and lost no
time in fleeing for his life towards Oughterard.

One of the few landlords who led a company of United recruits
to Castlebar was John Moore of Ballintaffy (midway between
Claremorris and Kiltimagh). Four years previously, John Moore,
with his landlord neighbours, John Joyce of Oxford House and
Thomas Ormsby of Ballinamore, sat on the jury that found
'Fighting' Fitzgerald guilty of the murder of another landlord,
Randal McDonnell of Windsor House, Castlebar.

The High Sheriff of Mayo, Denis Browne, saw in Fitzgerald (an
influential landlord and nephew of Thomas Hervey, the Earl of
Bristol and bishop of Derry) an enemy to be eliminated at all costs
and he did not hide his happiness when Fitzgerald was executed.
Browne was to become one of the most execrated individuals in
Irish history because of the ruthless way in which he put down all
attempts at rebellion in the wake of the defeat at Ballinamuck. He
was known far and wide as Donncha an Rópa (Denis of the Rope).

Seeing one of his hand-picked jurors side with the rebels led him
to have a secret tunnel constructed between his house (now the
Convent of Mercy in Claremorris) and a grove of trees some distance away as an escape route in case of a rebel victory.

During their march from Castlebar to Ballinamuck, the French
and Irish force marched through Bohola direct to Swinford. The
Castlebar–Swinford main road at that time joined the Swinford–

Kiltimagh main road at Carrabawn, a mile from Swinford, and it was on this road that General Humbert entered Swinford.

When a historian, Dr Hayes, travelled to Castlebar and Swinford, and retraced Humbert's march to Longford nearly fifty years ago, he was wrongly informed regarding the route taken. He was told in Swinford that Humbert marched to Foxford and then to Swinford. Such a route would involve a detour of 15 or 16 miles, two unnecessary crossings of the River Moy and a march through mountain foothills, which would be ideal ambush terrain for enemy units. This, to seasoned campaigners like Humbert or Blake, the Irish commander, would have been unthinkable. General Humbert and his aides, Sarrazin and Charcot, dined in Anthony Corley's Hotel, now O'Hare's, on the square in Swinford.

The French leader first called a halt and, after sentries were posted and scouting parties sent out, ordered the troops into a large field, part of which is now the grounds of the vocational school. Two steers donated by Brabazon (the local landlord) and two more donated by or taken from the Bohola landlord McManus were hastily prepared and roasted. Four large iron gates belonging to Brabazon were used as roasting grids over large turf fires. Having eaten, the troops marched on to Bellaghy, where they spent the night. There, one of their flanking parties, sent out the day before leaving Castlebar, rode up with the news that large enemy forces lay directly between them and the River Shannon.

This prompted Humbert to change course in the hope of outflanking his enemies and getting into the central plain and, hopefully, on to Dublin via the upper reaches of the Shannon. He marched his men northwards, hoping to find a crossing on the Shannon that was unguarded. Meanwhile, an English army was advancing from Sligo to confront him under the command of Colonel Vereker, an ancestor of Lord Mountbatten.

Unfortunately for Humbert, there was an orchard in the vicinity of the site where the army rested for the night. The apples were unripe, but the French soldiers were ravenous by this time and ate all that they could find. The consequences were predictable. The next morning the vast majority were in no condition to confront

Vereker as they were suffering from what could politely be called Montezuma's revenge.

In the ensuing engagement, Humbert's men were suffering heavy casualties as the English held an advantageous position and they had a field piece that was causing havoc in the French lines. Then, in a feat of outstanding courage, Bartholomew Teeling, an Irishman and a captain in Humbert's army, rode forth, zigzagging to dodge the bullets, and managed to get close enough to the gunner to shoot him dead.

At that, Vereker fell back and retreated as far as Ballyshannon in Donegal. It is unclear why Vereker faltered in his resolve when the gunner was shot or why he retreated as far north as Ballyshannon. Humbert found an unguarded crossing at Ballintra Bridge, south of Lough Allen, and the Franco-Irish force swung south, heading for Granard.

Teeling was captured when Humbert lay down his sword at Ballinamuck and unconditionally surrendered. He tried to have Teeling treated as a French officer and given prisoner-of-war status, but his pleas were in vain and Teeling was hanged as a traitor to the Crown. A street in nearby Tubbercurry bears his name. There is also an adjoining street named after General Humbert.

Meanwhile, the United Irishmen of Longford and Westmeath had assembled. They captured Wilson's Hospital near Mullingar, but failed to take the town of Granard. Humbert, on hearing of the midlands, rising decided to link up with the insurgents there and headed straight for Granard. He abandoned some of the heavier guns so as to travel at greater speed. So far he had eluded the cordon closing in around him. With some luck, he hoped to slip past the net, reach Granard and then strike for Dublin, which was virtually unprotected as most of the garrison has been moved to Connacht. Humbert was in a perilous position as General Cornwallis, with an immensely superior army, was straight in front of him, blocking his attempt to link up with the United Irishmen who had rebelled, while General Lake was closing in from the rear. The Franco-Irish force was like meat in a proverbial sandwich.

They had got as far as Cloone in South Leitrim, where scouts brought the news to Humbert that Cornwallis was 5 miles away at Mohill, blocking his way to Granard, and Lake, with an army of equal size, was closing in from the rear.

Humbert realised that he was surrounded and outnumbered, but decided to push on, even though the best he could do then was to offer token resistance before surrender. The skirmish took place at Ballinamuck in County Longford. The French surrendered after half an hour of desultory skirmishing and then, with their honour satisfied, Humbert ordered his men to lay down their arms. The French were treated as prisoners of war but the Irish were shown no mercy.

Left to fight on their own, their stubborn resistance earned tributes from some of their enemies. The French force at Ballinamuck has been estimated at about 900 men. There are no definite figures of the Irish casualties in this battle, although it is believed that 300 died, 400 were taken as prisoners and another 400 escaped. However, with martial law and unauthorised killings by the victors being a regular pattern of life in Ireland for three years or more after the rising, it is, of course, impossible to accurately estimate the number of casualties connected with that Continental invasion of Ireland.

It must also be remembered that records were scant and unreliable, especially in relation to Tone's 'men of no property', who were not fully regarded as human beings by the victorious, occupying army.

2

THE AFTERMATH

Writers have often commented on the difficulty of obtaining reliable information on events connected with the '98 Rising in the west of Ireland in comparison to County Wexford and other Leinster counties. Unfortunately, the reason for this is the famine. In Mayo and in the west in general, whole villages, with all their history, folklore and customs, were wiped out. The famine did not make such an impact on more prosperous, thinly populated counties like Wexford, Wicklow, Carlow and Kildare. Many farms in those counties remain in the possession of direct descendants of people who took part in or witnessed events connected with the 1798 Rising.

Many of the Mayo men who escaped from the massacre of Ballinamuck were Gaelic speakers and were between 150 and 200 miles from their native heath. To add to their woes, the River Shannon lay between them and home, and it was well watched and guarded to prevent their return. Ill-clad and ill-shod, with winter around the corner, their lot was not a happy one. There is a tale of a Shannon boatman who rowed two loads of Mayo men across the river one night shortly after the fight of Ballinamuck.

Only on his deathbed a few years later, could he dare to mention the matter as blood money and spies were plentiful for years after '98. There was another story of a Roscommon woman living near the Shannon in 1798, who, on a few occasions, found her cows milked dry when she collected them for the morning milking. She was afraid to mention the matter to anyone, as she guessed that it meant that some Mayo rebels had passed during the night or early morning.

In 1798, the summer and autumn were finer than average and all the hay and grain crops were collected early. However, the potato stalks remained green until mid-October; this was the favourite hiding ground for the hunted rebels during the day and they travelled all night.

To make matters worse, most of them had to discard their pikes as they were too noticeable and unwieldy. It is no wonder that a high proportion of the Mayo insurgents are listed as 'never returned'. A few of the insurgents were men who deserted from the Redcoats or militia regiments and when caught, whether armed or not, their fate was sealed. Leaders like General Blake of Garracloon, Colonel O'Dowd of Bonniconlon and Colonel Bellew of Killala, all trained veteran soldiers, were executed without any semblance of a trial.

Colonel McDonnell of Carracon, who was wounded at the capture of Castlebar, escaped to France, was refused promotion by Napoleon and so went to America, where he died. One of the Murrisk Abbey friars who joined the United men (insurgents), Fr Michael Gannon, escaped to France in a French officer's uniform and rose to a high rank in the French army. The other friar, Myles Prendergast, escaped to Connemara along with Johnny Gibbons and a few more United Irishmen.

Johnny Gibbons was captured by the Redcoats with the aid of a spy who had damped the powder in Johnny's pistols to ensure his downfall. When Johnny saw that his pistols were useless and that the house was encircled by his enemies, he exclaimed: '*Tá Johnny i nead lachain 'gus a mhéar i bpoll tráthair!*' (Johnny is in a duck's nest and his finger in an auger-hole!)

This saying survived and was used to describe anybody in a tight corner. Packing victims' fingers into grooved auger-holes was a form of punishment in those days and ducks' nests were so constructed that the ducks could not leave until released (duck eggs were too valuable as a food in those days of continuous privation to allow the ducks to lay out in ponds or rivers).

When Johnny Gibbons was executed in Castlebar, his godfather Denis Browne (Donncha an Rópa), took pleasure in being present, as he had when his sworn enemy, Fighting Fitzgerald, had been executed some years earlier.

Captain Mangan of Sion Hill was killed a few years after the rising, just as a free pardon was being prepared for a number of insurgents. Local tradition says that his fate was sealed by a spy who felled him with a stone after he had got through a ring of soldiers at Letter, near Nephin.

Among those listed as 'never returned' are John Moore of Ballintaffy, Henry Jordan of Rosslevin and Seamas Dubh Horkan of Rathscanlon, Swinford. (Henry Jordan is believed to have died in Connemara.)

Among those who went from Swinford with Seamas Dubh Horkan to join up in Castlebar were Paddy Brennan, a blacksmith who forged the pikes for the local United Irishmen, and Seamas 'Taillúir' (Tailor) Durkin. Durkin had his workshop in what is now the local garda station. His grandfather was a landlord, locally known as Muiris na Muaidh (Maurice of the Moy). Muiris lived a half mile south of Cloonacanana ford on the River Moy. The walls of his dwelling still stand close to the main Swinford–Aclare road.

Muiris na Muaidh was the landlord of the nine townlands nearest to Cloonacanana ford. He fought as a young officer in the Jacobite army at Aughrim, one of the bloodiest battles in Irish history. After Aughrim, he lost most of his lands in the Williamite confiscations. Admittedly he was not fighting for Ireland's freedom. He was fighting, like his commander, Patrick Sarsfield, Earl of Lucan, for the right of the poltroon English King James II to rule Ireland instead of William of Orange. Incidentally, he was, of course, fighting for his landed estates. Ironically, the Vatican supported William of Orange.

Seamas Durkin escaped from the massacre of Ballinamuck and found refuge in a disused sandpit in a large field, from which he saw the Redcoats searching along the hedgerows around the field. After nightfall, he headed in an easterly direction, luckily for himself, as all roads to the west were well watched. After some days, he found shelter and employment with a farmer in a quiet spot 30 miles from

Ballinamuck. Some time afterwards, he went back to his old trade and worked as a journeyman tailor as he moved from place to place.

It was almost three years after '98 before he returned home. He re-opened his tailor's shop at first, but friends advised him to close it down and leave the town, as spies were still on the lookout for easy money and the townspeople of Swinford were loyal to the Crown. He heeded their advice and built a small house in the townland of Cloonacanana, beside the old fort of Lisconnell.

He married a few years later and I can remember his two daughters, Nellie and Winnie. Winnie married a local man, Tom Salmon, and Nellie married Martin Henry of Ballydrum, my paternal grandfather. Grandmother Nellie never fully mastered the English language, but for a torrent of invectives in Gaelic she was hard to beat. When she died in 1912, she was nearly 100 years old.

Two Mayo priests were executed for complicity, or aiding and abetting the insurgents. Father Manus Sweeney of Achill was executed on the market crane in Newport and Fr Conroy of Addergoole in Castlebar. Another priest, Fr Owen Cowley, died from ill health and hardship while on the run. The tree in the Mall on which Fr Conroy was executed was blown down by a storm in 1918. At a huge county anti-conscription meeting in the Mall a few days later, De Valera referred to the tree and its history, having been briefed on the matter by local republicans.

The priests who sided with the rebels in 1798 were excommunicated. To this day it is believed the fiat or excommunication edict has not been revoked.

3

GREAT-GRANDMOTHER'S TALES

My maternal great-grandmother, who died in 1911 and to the best of her reckoning was 102 years old, was a mine of information regarding events connected with the famine. Unfortunately, nobody thought of recording her tales of her early days.

Her husband Thomas McDonnell of Ballintaffy, Claremorris, died a young man in 1847, leaving her with a very young family. In keeping with local custom, the Widow McDonnell was known all her life by her maiden name, Mary McHugh. Her holding of land, being a middleman's holding, was larger than the average and this she regarded as being more of a liability than an asset as the annual rent to her landlord, Ormsby of Ballinamore, was correspondingly high.

At the time of her husband's death, she had four cottiers as small sub-letters on her holding. Each cottier rented one field with his cottage and tilled it to the utmost. The size of the field varied from 1 to 2 acres. Milk was usually supplied by the landowner who let the cottage and field, in return for seasonal assistance with spring and harvesting work.

Her landlord allowed her to increase the number of sub-letters to eight. This, she maintained, was the difference between security and eviction for her. Their small rents, plus the assistance they gave her on the farm as required, almost paid her rent to the landlord.

She told a rather interesting tale involving her husband.

Sometime after their marriage, he went to Dublin to lodge some money in a bank, there being no provincial barks at the time. One of his horses was lame and the other one, a mare, was rearing a foal, so he set off walking at daybreak on a fine summer morning. Sometime on the second day, having crossed the Shannon, he got a lift from two men on a horse-drawn miller's dray or low-slung cart. He found that his companions could not speak Irish. Luckily for himself, he could understand English much better than he could speak it. Between their hints and whispers, he picked up enough of their conversation to realise that they meant to rob and kill him, if necessary, when they came to the wood beyond the next little town. He had donned a new suit and shoes leaving home and this led his companions to believe that he was worth robbing.

He planned to jump off the dray when they reached the town. Hearing an unusual animal-like roar, he looked ahead and saw a drover and a bunch of donkeys approaching along the road. On spotting the horse, one donkey ran forward, braying loudly.

The horse wheeled around on the road and bolted in the opposite direction at top speed. My great-grandfather leaped off the dray and over the fence into a nearby field. He had never seen a donkey before, and judging by their blood-curdling braying, he felt it would be better to get out of their reach as fast as possible. The drover, however, hailed him and assured him that his animals were harmless. Seeing a donkey was an experience for him as donkeys were almost unknown in Mayo at the time.

The Napoleonic wars left Ireland almost denuded of horses, which were snapped up for the imperial cavalry regiments, so English and Scottish donkey dealers saw a ready market in Ireland. They shipped

the donkeys in their thousands over the short Larne–Stranraer route in flat-bottom boats.

My great-grandfather called to a farmhouse shortly afterwards and stayed there overnight. He continued his journey at daybreak the next morning and took care not to fall in with his carter companions again.

The McDonnells kept a bull. In Irish farming circles, a bull rated nearly as high as a hunter or a racehorse as a status symbol. One of the most sustaining foods in those famine days, a mixture of oatmeal and blood known as *preasán fola*, was expected to sustain a hard-working man for a full day. (A mixture of oatmeal and milk was known as *preasán* and a mixture of oatmeal and butter, which could be moulded into cakes or rolls, was known as *bustán*. It was said that this was the staple diet of Humbert's army.)

In the McDonnell household, the bull bore the brunt of the bleeding rituals. For some reason, the bleeding operation was always carried out on Sunday afternoons. The widow said that her bull became so accustomed or resigned to the ritual that he uttered the most mournful bellows when he saw his tormentors approaching.

Bleeding was effected by puncturing a vein in the animal's left shoulder. On the final occasion (for the bull), the operation was carried out by a son of the regular vet, who was ill. Through some miscalculation, the bleeding could not be stopped and in the excitement the bull broke loose and quickly bled to death from over-exertion.

The widow decided to make the best of a bad job. She sent to Claremorris for a regular butcher and got the bull prepared and salted.

She found that she had to send a man on horseback to Kisallagh, Westport, for a bag of salt as she could only get pinches of it locally. The man who sold the salt was known as a panner. He got it from trapped seawater using what was known as the shallow-pan method. Having salted most of the animal, she found she had enough left to make a feast for her cottiers, relatives and neighbours. That feast, and what they took home, got them through the hungriest spring she ever remembered – 1848.

Watercress was a highly prized piece of food in the famine years. A broad, sluggish drain where watercress abounded, midway along the Claremorris–Kiltimagh road, was mentioned by the Widow McDonnell as being black with people eating this plant in the famine years. The edible root of a herb known as the *blioscán* was dug up and eaten raw, as was another herb root known as the *cútharlán*, which had a marble-sized bulb on the root.

My great-grandmother had vivid memories of turbulent elections and bye-elections around the famine years and later. The candidates, all landlords, were adept at rousing the starving peasantry. In the words of James Connolly, 'They engendered as much heat as was possible into the part of the body politic furthest removed from the idea of social justice.'

In one election, Lord Oranmore and Browne, the Tory candidate, was opposed by Kirwan, a Catholic landlord with repeal sympathies. After 1848, the year of revolutions around the world and the first incipient attempts at democratic upsurge, the English government passed a law that made a defeated election candidate accountable for the victorious candidate's election expenses.

This in itself was a blow against democracy, as it ensured that only men of substance could seek election. When Lord Oranmore opened his election campaign in Claremorris, he had a kinsman, a son of Donncha an Rópa, on his platform. A local clergyman, Fr Gibbons, led a group who broke up the meeting, shouting 'soap the rope' at young Browne. This was one of his father's nicknames.

Lady Oranmore, seeing the election tide flowing against her husband, went to Archbishop McHale and begged him on her knees to turn the tide in favour of her husband. Her husband went around, saying that the branches of his trees would pay for the election if he lost.

Kirwan replied by saying that the hooves and horns of all his cattle would more than pay for the election. Lady Oranmore, however, realised that her husband was an encumbered landlord. Archbishop McHale acceded to her request and threw his weight behind Oranmore, who won the election. Dr McHale lived to regret his action, as Oranmore proved a strong opponent of any scheme designed to benefit the plain, hard-working masses.

Old Animal Charms and Cures

T wo miles west of Bohola, along the main road to Castlebar, lies the townland of Loughkeeraun. The tiny bogland lough or lake, from which the townland got its name, has completely disappeared over the past half century owing to local drainage operations. There was an old tradition, which held that St Kieran cured a valuable cow that was dying with water taken from the lough and, because of this, the lough was a popular place of pilgrimage for centuries.

Pilgrims came to Loughkeeraun mainly to pray for luck and prosperity with their livestock in the forthcoming year. Not to be outdone in religious fervour, some pilgrims took rolls of butter to throw into the lake as an offering to the saint.

More practical local people came later and salvaged the rolls of butter. Having recycled the butter, it was packed into their butter firkins and sold at the Swinford butter market. I can remember pilgrims going to Loughkeeraun on 15 August, which seemed to be the most popular date of all for local pilgrimages in this country.

For a kicking cow, a popular cure was to get two people to pass a burning sod of turf under and over the standing cow in the names of saints Patrick, Bridget and Colmcille. For a newly calved heifer cow to give butter-rich milk, a similar ritual was performed. In this case, the lighted turf sod was passed around the cow's back legs in the names of the Blessed Trinity.

I remember on one occasion, while assisting an aunt in this operation, the cow showed her disapproval by kicking the burning sod

into a bundle of straw, almost setting fire to the byre. Having been rebuked for laughing, I was told that the fire was blessed. However, I felt that the ritual was more of pagan than Christian origin. In some districts, up to the present day, giving away milk on May Day was forbidden as it was believed that doing so would mean giving away one's luck for the rest of the year.

Giving away fire on that day was also taboo. I recall a story by an old neighbouring woman who absent-mindedly went to borrow coal on May morning when she found her fire had gone out. Her return trip was made in record time, without the coal of fire.

Some years ago, I called on a well-known County Mayo chemist for a remedy for calf scour. I mentioned to him that in my neighbourhood, people of old had great faith in the soup of boiled briar roots for this ailment. The chemist said that tannin was a popular agent for contracting the lower bowel to arrest scour. Briar root, he said, contained a high percentage of tannin.

In bygone times, beef and butter were the most important items in rural economy – as they are at the present time. Anybody found trespassing on a neighbour's land on May Day might be suspected of gathering certain lucky herbs in order to take the neighbour's luck.

If the trespasser could be heard saying the words '*Im agus bainne dom*' (Butter and milk to me) when plucking herbs on another man's land, he was in real danger.

The use of the dead hand to bring luck in butter-gathering is happily a thing of the past. The last known instance of anything in that line being practised in Mayo was over 100 years ago at the place where the three parishes of Killedan, Knock and Kilcolman join, almost midway between Claremorris, Kiltimagh and Knock. An old woman who lived alone was being waked in the year 1850. A fearsome thunderstorm sprang up during the night, which so frightened all at the wake that they rushed out and away home. When some of them returned the following morning, they found that the old woman's right hand had been severed and taken away. I heard this tale being told by an old man, John Hynes, over fifty years ago. His father was one of those who attended the old woman's wake.

In some cases, animal help was invoked to cure human ailments. Donkey's milk and ferret's leavings, together with the fasting spit and boiled primroses, were time-honoured cures for jaundice and other mysterious complaints. Some of those confirm the saying about the cure being worse than the ailment.

Scrawing and Burning

I n the short spell between the famine years of 1845–48 and the repeal of the Corn Laws by the British government in 1851, the peasants of Ireland changed their practices in a big way and began to grow grain crops, chiefly oats. They saw the futility of relying too much on the potato as a main tillage crop. Unfortunately, they continued and intensified an old custom connected with tillage known as 'scrawing and burning', which involved cutting away or stripping the top grassy or heathery sods of the field intended for cultivation.

Those surface sods or scraws were dried and piled into heaps which were set afire and allowed to smoulder to heaps of ashes. The ashes were later spread on the land in the mistaken belief that it was a first-class fertilizer. This practice, as time proved, only impoverished the land.

Forty years ago, a man named John Drudy, who was well versed in local history and traditions, showed me fields in his native village of Glann, Charlestown, to prove a point. He said the fields in question, after nearly 100 years of good care and treatment, were only beginning to recover from the effects of scrawing and burning.

The skimming off of the tough surface scraws with heavy spades or loys was hard and laborious work, and it was in vain.

I heard a local joke about a father and son that had spent the whole day scrawing and came in to their evening meal around nightfall. This meal and a breakfast, of which two boiled duck eggs

apiece were the main feature, were all there was in the way of suste-
nance in those times. There were no tea breaks or other perks of that
kind. The father and son's main meal was a large plate of Indian meal
porridge laid down between them. This Indian meal was generally
known as 'yella buck'. The son sat down first and as the stirabout was
hot, he began skimming off the cooler outside part with his spoon.
When the father mentioned this, the son replied, 'I can be scrawing,
Father, and you can be burning.'

At that time, distilleries and malting houses were a feature of the
economic life of many provincial towns in Ireland. At the malting
houses, the grain was bought from the farmers and prepared for the
distilleries. While not absorbing nearly as much of the grain grown in
the country as the mills, they helped to stabilise prices.

The repeal of the Corn Laws in 1851 was a cruel blow just as economic conditions were slowly improving after the disastrous famine.
This law allowed the dumping of foreign grain into the country, free
of tax or any restrictions.

This grain, chiefly Indian corn and meal from the United States
and wheat from Canada imported at low prices, put many Irish
millers out of business and also most of the distilleries and malting houses. Oat production declined and emigration from Ireland,
which had been slowing down, began to rise again.

One of the last malting houses in Mayo to close was located in
Upper Mount Street, Claremorris. Some years before they closed,
they advertised in a Dublin newspaper for an experienced maltster.
A Dublin man who gave the name of Doyle got the job. He proved
to be very talkative and boastful over his drinks. As the first effects of
famine began to be felt, he openly advocated rebellion as the only
remedy left to the people. He told them of how he had been out
in 1798 and in 1803 with Robert Emmet. He would dramatically
exclaim, with a far-away look in his eyes, 'Ah! Them were the days!'

The local parson in Claremorris at the time was the Revd Darcy
Sirr. He was a son of the notorious British army town major in
Dublin around 1798, Major Sirr, who did more than his share in
the rounding-up of Lord Edward Fitzgerald and the '98 leaders in
Dublin and played a similar role with Robert Emmet and his com-

rades five years later. Having heard the maltster Doyle blowing his trumpet on one occasion, the Revd Darcy Sirr felt that he had seen the man and heard the voice before. By degrees, it dawned on him that he had seen the man many years ago in his father's house handling some papers with the major.

He also remembered that the man's name was Duggan. He searched among his father's papers, most of which he had taken with him to Mayo. (He later gave those papers over to be filed away or published as the authorities saw fit.)

When he found the papers he felt would clear up the identity of Doyle, alias Duggan, he sent for the man in question, saying he would be obliged if he called on the following Sunday to his house. When the maltster called, the parson told him to be seated while he went to his study. When he returned, he laid a paper before his visitor on the table. Pointing to a signature at the foot of the document, he said, 'Do you recognise that signature, Duggan?'

Duggan seemed stunned for a few moments. He then stood up and went silently out, returned to town and then turned left on the Ballyhaunis road and probably continued on to Dublin. He was never seen in Claremorris again.

The document the Revd Darcy Sirr laid before Duggan was an acknowledgement of having on a certain date received the sum of 50 guineas from Major Sirr for information which helped in the capture of Robert Emmet. The document carried the signature of James Duggan and was counter-signed by Major Sirr. Incidentally, a few years later, another man connected with the 1803 uprising drifted to Mayo. Barney Moran, Robert Emmet's executioner, came to Mayo a penniless mendicant. Despised and disowned by the government he served so slavishly, he died in Ballina workhouse fifty years after Emmet's Rising.

THE BELLMEN

Up to forty years ago, nearly every town in Ireland could boast one or more town criers or bellmen, as they were more generally called. Now they are quickly becoming only a memory. It seems strange that a segment of the community with so many colourful characters in its ranks down through the years can recede into the past all but unnoticed.

Nowadays, with more advance notices and an ever-increasing amount of advertising in newspapers, television and radio, public address systems, printed handbills, etc., the crier or bellman is no longer required to 'get the message across', to use a modern slang phrase. It seems possible that the criers may have been part of the economic life of the country for at least 200 years in their own way.

When the French invasion force landed at Kilcummin in 1798, the town crier in Ballina, 8 miles away, announced in the streets of Ballina a few hours later that Napoleon had landed near Killala. A month later, when Lord Roden's Foxhunters and other Redcoat troops returned to retake Ballina and Killala, the Ballina crier was arrested. He would have shared the fate of the United men, Walsh, Barrett and others who had been executed, only that an officer of the notorious North Mayo Militia vouched that he was 'stupid and harmless' and would believe any story he was told.

One of my earliest recollections is listening to a Swinford crier, Patsy Cox, locally known as

Patcheen, ringing his bell and announcing the coming of a circus to town. Patsy Cox was a child of 3 years when the famine hit Swinford in 1847. He was taken to Swinford workhouse, together with his parents, all stricken down with the dreaded fever that left little hope for famine victims. Two or three days later, he was carried out with a dozen more to be buried in a mass grave. After the first shovelful of earth was flung in on top of the victims, the infant Patsy stirred his feeble hand slightly. Luckily, one of the grave attendants noticed the movement and took him back to the workhouse. He recovered and grew up to be a fit, able youngster, as he got better inmate treatment by the workhouse staff, who regarded his escape from death and burial as a miracle.

Over 500 famine victims were buried in mass graves in an elevated spot beside the modern Swinford hospital. Those victims came from the Swinford Poor Law Union Area, which embraced all East Mayo and extended to the Lung River in County Roscommon at that time.

In the closing years of the last century and the opening decades of the present century, a keen rivalry existed in Kiltimagh between two local bellmen: John Forde, better known as Jack Straw, and Tom McNicholas, known as Tom Thrasher. The latter got his nickname because of his father, who was a noted thresher of oats with the old-time flail.

The flail, now passing into the limbo of forgotten things, consisted of a 5 foot by 1¼-inch stick called a *colpán*, which was loosely attached to a shorter stick known as a *buailteán* or beater. The two sticks were tied together with a tie of leather or a strip of calico cloth called a *fuang*. Grasping the *colpán* firmly in his hands, the thresher swung the *buailteán* over his head in a circular motion to give impetus to the blow before bringing it down on the head of the sheaf to be threshed. The most satisfactory wood for the *colpán* was said to be holly; for the *buailteán*, hazel.

One of the Celtic legends of old mentions St Patrick meeting Oisín from the old Fenian school of warriors. Among other things, St Patrick showed Oisín his father, Oscar, busily threshing the devils in Hell. Every time he had the devils well cornered for better results, the *fuang* of his flail snapped and he had to start all over again. As

Oisín stood watching, St Patrick said he would grant him one wish, expecting he would ask that Oscar be delivered from the lower regions.

Oisín immediately replied, 'I wish Oscar had a *fuang* on his flail that would never break.'

Tom Thrasher's father threshed a good-sized stack of oats daily, with Tom turning the sheaves for him, and their combined pay was four shillings and two meals per day.

Jack Straw was a less aggressive type and had spent a short term in college in his youth. During the Land War days, ballads applauding the fight of the tenants and condemning the landlords and the authorities were classed as insurrectionary. Copies of those ballads were printed on sheets of paper and sold at fairs and other mass meetings for a halfpenny each.

To prevent the circulation of those seditious songs, the Royal Irish Constabulary (RIC) was ordered to prevent the ballad singers and vendors selling those leaflets. Bellmen were the chief sellers of ballads, with other side-lines such as peddling matches, shoelaces, pins and needles and other everyday household necessities in order to eke out a living.

John Forde circumvented the government order by carrying a bunch of oaten straw for which he charged his ballad customers a halfpenny each, giving them a free ballad and saying at the same time, 'I'll sell my straw and I'll defy the law.' This is how he got the name Jack Straw. During the Boer War years, Jack was progressive enough to get a peep show lantern, which showed pictures of the war and the combatants, for which he charged a halfpenny a peep.

On one occasion, the Kiltimagh bellman, Padneen Kane, told Tom Thrasher that he had a good mind to get married and asked for his advice.

Tom said, 'You have no house or land, not even a garden, and I suppose you have no money?'

'No,' replied Padneen.

Having pretended to give the problem serious consideration, Tom said, 'Go ahead and get married; you can't be much worse off than you are!'

ACHILL BREEZES

I spent the winter months of 1939/40 on Achill Island supervising road construction, bridge construction and repairs to piers and boat slips on behalf of Mayo County Council. The Second World War was gaining momentum at the time and travel was becoming more difficult as cars, petrol, bicycles and spare parts were harder to obtain. I remember my first 60-mile bicycle journey to Achill, with a good stiff wind in my face. Between Mulranny and Achill, I caught up with a tramp locally known as Pateen. As I was making slow progress cycling against the strong wind, I decided to walk and enjoy his company to Achill.

Observing some men digging around a telegraph pole, I told my companion that they must now be lifting up the line of telegraph poles as the railway line had been closed down and the rails lifted a short time previously. 'Well, indeed,' said the tramp, 'they could leave them alone because those poles were the only biteen of shelter they have in Achill.'

Seeing me laugh at the idea of shelter from telegraph poles, he said, 'I was fooled once when I was depending on those poles for shelter.' Pointing to a densely populated village close to the old railway line, the tramp said, 'That village down there is Shruffaun and a nice friendly old crowd live down there. I seldom pass this way without calling down to see them. One dark morning after leaving that village with a good sup of *poitín* inside me, I mistook one of those poles for the trunk of a tree and I sat down and put my back to it. I fell asleep for a couple of hours and only realised that it wasn't a tree at all when I woke up and it was broad daylight.'

Meeting an old man on the road, the tramp stood back to exchange a few words with him and then re-joined me with a broad smile. 'If you don't mind,' he said, 'that poor devil has got it in his head to get married.'

'I admire his courage,' said I.

'Courage?' scoffed the tramp. 'You could call it the *biseach chun báis*.' (This is an Achill saying meaning the improvement before death.)

When I parted with my companion after a drink at Achill Sound, he said, 'We must soldier on to the end of the road, brother, and we should never worry too much about anything.'

I really envied his ability to look on life and its problems so lightly. Around this time, the famous swing bridge at Achill Sound had been declared unfit to carry heavy traffic. One result of this was that two heavy stone-crushing plants intended for road works in Achill planned by Mayo County Council could not travel to the island. All the broken stones required for road-making in Achill had to be by hand with 8oz hammers. The stones had to be broken small enough to pass through an iron ring 3 inches in diameter, which was used occasionally for spot checks. Each man's pile of broken stone was shovelled through a wooden measure to determine tonnage.

The pay rate was four shillings per ton of broken stone and the men were limited to three days' work per week. If a man had been in receipt of twelve shillings or over per week in unemployment assistance (dole), he could claim four days' work per week. To crown it all, the stone was hard blue granite. All the bleakest and most windswept roads in Achill were staffed with stonebreakers when the scheme got underway.

The Shraheen, Dooega, Keel-Dugort, Dooagh and Bunnacurry Valley roads resembled British Empire building at its most pernicious in North-West India as we read about it or saw it in pictures. One day I was sizing up the depressing sight of gangs of fine specimens of Irish manhood seated on piles of wet stones on the Shraheen road, hammering away at the unrelenting granite and gneiss rocks. I was roused from my daydreams by the local parish priest.

He told me he had called to know if there was any cursing by the workmen on the job. 'Oh, yes, father,' I replied facetiously, 'the finest cursing I ever heard in any part of the world.'

He told me that cursing was one of the worst sins and that I should not allow it. I replied that I was not so sure that it was a sin at all. I quoted the biblical passage about our Lord cursing the fig tree for not bearing fruit out of season. 'You must realise,' said the parish priest, 'that he was our Lord and he could do as he liked.'

I concluded by saying that apart from breaking the stones to size, the men could do as they liked as far as I was concerned. After the good father departed, I began to wonder what reasons he would have given for all the cursing mentioned in *The Tripartite Life of Saint Patrick*, the cursing of Tara by St Ruadhan or the litany of curses attributed to St Colmcille, who, if we are to believe legend, must be the greatest fulminator of curses among all the Irish saints.

While residing at the foot of Tonragee Mountain in 1938, I climbed the mountain one fine evening in spring. A companion, a local youth, gave me the history attached to a cairn of flagstones on the mountain summit. The cairn was known as Leachtaí Lytell.

Father Manus Sweeney, a native of Dookinella in the lower part of Achill Island, was executed in Newport on the day of the August Fair there in 1799 after a sham trial for complicity in the 1798 Rebellion. His having been educated in France and his good knowledge of the French language went a long way towards securing his conviction by the judicial minions of English imperialism, especially after the ill-fated French invasion of Mayo the previous year.

When Fr Manus mounted the scaffold, one of the onlookers was a native of the Protestant colony in Dugort, Achill. The man's name was Lytell and he had attended the fair that day with two companions. Lytell, who had a fair knowledge of the Irish language and wanted to show his bigotry and hatred of priests, exclaimed, '*Tá splíonach shagairt ag eirí go h-ard inniu.*' (Priest's flesh is rising high today.)

A sister of Fr Manus who knew Lytell well (or, according to another account, Fr Manus himself) turned to Lytell and told him not to be so brave or bold; that his own end would come some day and that he might not have so many witnesses to sympathise with him. Father Manus was executed on the market crane in Newport, which stood on the market square until twenty years ago. Executing political prisoners on fair days or occasions of public assembly was a ritual of the British calculated to strike terror into the greatest number of people.

After the execution, Lytell and his two friends retired to a local alehouse and later set out on foot for home, around 28 miles away. As they approached the village of Tonragee, a thick fog came in from Bellacraher Bay and the three travellers became separated in the fog.

Two of them arrived in the colony on the following day, but there was no trace of Lytell. Several days later, the dogs in Tonragee were observed coming down off the mountain, carrying human bones. A search party that followed them on their next journey up the mountain found all that remained of Lytell and flung together the mound of stones to mark the spot.

Having heard the tale, I wondered what unseen compelling force caused Lytell to climb the steep side of Tonragee Mountain, 1,500 feet above Bellacraher Bay, and perish there alone.

WINDOW ON THE PAST

Before the Claremorris–Swinford–Collooney railway line was opened in 1895, Swinford had been a leading provincial market town for the sale of farm produce, chiefly butter, pigs and oats for 100 years. The repeal of the Corn Laws around 1850 adversely affected oat production; afterwards, the pig and the butter firkin became the small tenant's standby to pay his landlord's rent. The ford over the river at Mill Street in Swinford was a Mecca on fair mornings for hundreds of steaming pigs. Having been walked several miles to market, they wallowed and washed themselves at this ford. Hence the name Swineford, later shortened to Swinford.

In those days, pigs were not sold until they were twelve months old. In summer, when the previous year's potato crop ran out and before the new potato crop was harvested, they were often fed on

green foods (cabbage, grass, coarse docks and other edible weeds) and were able to walk for miles to market. After a fair in Swinford, droves of pigs were walked to the ports of Ballina, Sligo and Newport. An old man told me he often saw scores of pigs being driven after the pig fairs in Swinford over the old Barnacoogue–Orlar–Carrowbehy route to Castlerea railway station.

The Swinford butter market attracted buyers from Sligo, Ballina, Westport, Newport and Killala, and suppliers from all across East Mayo and South Sligo.

At the market, tailors were on hand to measure you for a suit of home-spun frieze. Cobblers measured your feet if required for a pair of comfortable boots guaranteed to give two years of 'honest wear'. As late as 1941, I saw this at the fair in Achill Sound. At Swinford market in those days, there were spinning wheels, wheel- and hand-barrows, carts and cartwheels, chairs, stools and a straw-woven armchair called a *suisteóg*. Upholstered with horsehair or wool clippings, the *suisteóg* was regarded as a luxury.

Bundles of heather besoms, neatly tied and trimmed, were carried on the back from mountain districts and sold for a halfpenny each. W.H. Maxwell, in his book *Wild Sports of the West*, asserted that on a market day in Tuam, the number of beggars would outnumber the *lazzaroni* of Naples.

At one butter market in Swinford around 1880, a thousand firkins of butter were said to have been sold. As the gathering of one firkin of butter took months, this meant untold persevering, self-denial and drudgery for the housewife and her undernourished family.

At the marketplace, the butter buyers set up their tripod beam scales. Before being weighed or purchased, each firkin was pierced full length with an auger, which, when withdrawn, showed whether the butter was of uniform quality and colour. Prices were determined by this system of grading.

Afterwards, local carters took the firkins to some port, usually Ballina or Sligo. The carter's lot was not an easy one. If listed for Sligo, a convoy of carts left Swinford at around 5 a.m. Having delivered their loads at Sligo Quay, they collected a load of provisions to take back and tried to get to Ballinacarrow before nightfall, where they stayed overnight. In bad weather, they felt lucky to get to Ballysodare on their way home.

About fifty full- and part-time carters found employment in this way. John Bunyan, in his book *The Pilgrim's Progress*, describes Vanity Fair as a seductive mart where all the wares of the world were bawled out to hoodwink poor Christian and make him tarry or turn aside from his pilgrimage. Swinford market was just as thronged and miscellaneous. The spacious Main Street square was packed with tradesmen, handymen and pedlars of all kinds displaying their wares.

Coopers were there with tubs, firkins, piggins, noggins and churns; nailers with hand-wrought nails; tinsmiths with tin cans, saucepans and tinker's lamps. This last-named item was a globeless paraffin oil-burning contraption, giving off smoke and a smell out of all proportion to the sickly light produced. Nevertheless, with paraffin oil selling for a halfpenny a pint, it gradually replaced dip candles and bog deal 'splits' for domestic lighting.

In those days, in this respect, Swinford was not far behind Tuam, if it was behind at all. After the Napoleonic and Crimean wars, every garrison town in Ireland had its quota of ex-soldiers. These men, left without means of livelihood by their former masters, crowded into alleys and backstreets like the Lane in Swinford or *Bothar Garbh* in Claremorris. There, they created social problems that persisted until recent times. In those days there were knights of the road converging on the workhouses, ballad singers, travelling musicians and many other types of unfortunates. Petty robberies were a regular occurrence, so buyers and sellers ensured they were clear of woods and 'heel of the town' spots before dark. Then, as now, there was the gap between the 'haves' and the 'have-nots'. Gombeen men, as odious as the publicans of the Bible, grew fat by lending money. Crocks of yellow sovereigns were displayed on some shop windows in Swinford during and for many years after the famine, with the rate of interest and an exhortation to borrow displayed alongside them.

The interest rate of 5*d* per £1 seemed innocuous till the victim learned too late that this quotation meant 5*d* per month, or 25 per cent annually. Happily, this tribe of gombeen men have disappeared 'nor left a wrack behind'.

These jottings are indicative of the hard times that prevailed in Swinford and similar provincial market towns over the greater part of the last century.

9

THE NIGHT OF
THE BIG WIND

The most disastrous and terror-inspiring natural event in Irish history from 1798 to the famine was the storm that swept the country on the night of Sunday, 6 January, and the morning of 7 January 1839. It is believed that over seventy people were killed or drowned and well over 100 more died from exposure and hardships attributable to the storm.

Thousands were rendered homeless, boats were swamped or blown incredible distances inland and smashed to matchwood, and coaches were blown off the roads.

One group of Erris fishermen did not put to sea on that fateful night because, as they stoutly maintained later, they saw the *sí gaoithe* or storm spirit, a skeleton-like shadow with wildly waving arms silhouetted against a bank of sea fog.

Much of the destruction caused by the storm could have been avoided if the landlords had been more considerate towards their tenants. The tenants' dwellings would have been in better repair to withstand the storm, but every little improvement they carried out on their dwellings or farm buildings drew a reprisal from the landlord in the shape of an increase in their rent. In those days, petty country squires known as middlemen rented sections of the landlord's property, which they then sublet to tenants.

The storm of 1839 hit Swinford from the north-west, which was its exposed side as there was no railway station or sheltering railroad embankments at the time. Piles of thatch, slates, timbers and roofing flagstones blocked the streets. One street, Mill Street, was left without a single roof which had not been blown down. In its humble way, Mill Street was then the industrial sector of Swinford. Nailers, coopers, shoemakers, weavers, tailors and tinsmiths worked side-by-side in houses that have since disappeared.

One young man in Ballydrum village was so worried about his two stacks of oats – his only standby to pay his landlord's rent – that he got a ladder and climbed on to one stack and stayed there all through the storm to keep the stack from being blown away. His widowed mother climbed on to the other stack and did likewise. During the night, one fierce gust of wind swept her shawl away and it was found in Killaturly, 2 miles away. It was recognised thanks to a large shawl safety pin, which was a new innovation at the time. The shawl pin had been given to the old woman by the lady at the Big House as a gift for paying her rent so promptly. The pin, which was fastened, caused the shawl to balloon and be carried so far by the storm.

The threshing flail had only been introduced to the village a short time before the storm and before then the scutching stone was an important part of farm equipment. The old woman who lost her shawl said that the storm must have been sent as a punishment for adopting such a devil's emblem as the flail.

The Old Age Pensions Act, which granted pensions at the age of 70, became law in 1909, so anyone born on or before the night of the Big Wind automatically qualified for a pension. As no records of births or deaths were kept in 1839, or for many years afterwards, claimants had to appear before a pensions' official, magistrate or clergyman and satisfy him as to the genuineness of their claims.

Many children born around the time of the great storm had been told by their mothers that they were born on the night of the 'Big Wind'. The result was that the number claiming to have been born on that night was staggering. One priest in a parish near Swinford appointed a certain day on which to take particulars from pension claimants. When he found almost all the claimants saying that they were born on the night of the Big Wind, he exclaimed, 'It must have been the greatest storm since the beginning of the world if it blew you all into the world on the same night!'

One applicant from Swinford district told the pensions' officer that he well remembered the night of the Big Wind. Asked what he remembered about it, he said, 'I remember my mother blessing herself and shoving me and my cradle under the bed and saying the house would fall on us.'

'Surely,' said the pensions' officer, 'you don't expect me to believe that you remember what happened when you were in the cradle?' The old man told him that he was the youngest member of his family and that in his day the youngest child might have to sleep in the cradle for years owing to shortage of accommodation. He told the official that cradles were often made larger for that reason. The pensions' officer smilingly allowed his claim.

With modern buildings, stauncher and better sheltered farmsteads, and advance warnings of gales, it seems unlikely that the havoc and terror caused by the storm of 1839 could be repeated in this country.

10

AMUSEMENTS AT WAKES

Many theories have been advanced to explain the old Gaelic custom of playing games at wakes for the dead. All authorities agree that no disrespect for the dead was intended. Very often relatives of a deceased person asked the younger people at the wake to commence the games. Often an old man, feeling that his end was drawing near, gave instructions as to the games to be indulged in at his wake.

The old Gaelic race looked on a natural death as a happy release from the cares and worries of this world to a happier life in the next one. Only when a young person met a sudden or untimely end did they regard it as a cause for lamentation.

Until relatively recently, when the last sod of turf was cut, the last sheaf of grain reaped or some other seasonal work completed, God's mercy on the dead was invariably invoked by the people involved in the work.

When enjoying the first sample of some fruit or vegetable, such as new potatoes, the usual saying was, '*Go mbeirimid beo ag an am seo arís*' ('That we may be alive this time (next year) again'.)

I have often heard those invocations, which prove that consideration for the dead and thoughts of the hereafter were never far from the mind of the Gael.

East Mayo seems to have been one of the last Irish strongholds of the custom of playing games at wakes, as there are many people still alive who took part in them. The First World War and the Troubled Times helped to put an end to many old-world ideas.

Some of those games were just trials of strength or agility, such as tug-of-war with a brush handle over a chalked line on the floor, or jumping over and back across a stick while holding an end in each hand.

Two of the most popular games were known as *Thart an Bhróg* and 'Riding the Blind Donkey'. In the first named game, a number of players sat in a circle and secretly passed some small object to each other. A 'victim' seated on a chair in the centre of the circle was expected to name correctly who was in possession of the object when asked. The object was often a child's shoe and in order to mislead the man in the middle, the person in possession of the shoe would whisper, '*Chuir thart an bhróg*' ('pass the shoe'). This is how the game got its name.

In 'Riding the Blind Donkey', two stout kitchen chairs were placed about 4 feet apart. A strong spade or shovel handle was placed horizontally, with an end resting on the seat of each chair. The operator then had to sit cross-legged like a tailor on the spade handle. While precariously balanced there, four small objects, such as potatoes or small sods of turf, were placed on the outer corners of the chair seats and he was expected to knock those objects on to the floor with a short stick while maintaining his balance.

The penalties or forfeits for failure in those games varied in different localities. The penalty in *Thart an Bhróg* was usually a number of thumps on the back by the strong man of the company. As a concession, the victim might be allowed to hold his open hand, palm outwards, on his back to cushion the blows. In other places, the punishment might be a number of blows of a knotted straw rope. In 'Riding the Blind Donkey', the punishment was often to force a handful of *deannach* down the fallen jockey's back, between shirt and skin. *Deannach* was a dusty, abrasive by-product of oat milling, and as small oat mills dotted the countryside in those days, there was no shortage of the commodity. It caused a most unbearable itch on tender skin. Near Claremorris, a small lake bears the name of Loch na nDeannach owing to the *deannach* formerly dumped there.

An old man in South Mayo once told me of a game played at wakes around Claremorris in his youth. This game, which could hardly be called a parlour game, was known as *Bearradóir* (the shaver).

A number of young men lined up to be 'shaved'. Each was compelled to take a large mouthful of water and stand with distended cheeks while the barber or shaver gave him a mock shave with a goose or duck quill while intoning the words, '*Bearrfaidh mise mo sheandhuinín go lom, lom, lom*.' This implied that he would shave his client bare, bare, bare. If any client laughed, the rest squirted their mouthful of water in his face. Sometimes the unfortunate barber was on the receiving end when his client's mouthful of water exploded in his face.

The playing of those games was not always confined to wakes. Sometimes they were played on the night after a *meitheal*, assembled to help a backward neighbour with some seasonal work or when flax scutching or some such work was completed.

When the journeyman tailor came to a village, he usually billeted in some 'ready' house where there were no children to interfere with his work and where he often stayed the whole winter.

Owing to the poor lighting facilities in those days, it was work all day and play and yarns all night as people gathered to while away the long winter hours before bedtime. Years ago, in the village of Gleann Mhullaigh an Eo (Charlestown), I heard fragments of a local song to commemorate the visit of a journeyman tailor, Seán Bán Duffy, and his apprentice, Mullaney. One verse contained the lines:

There was cally for Mullaney and boxty for Seán Bán,
And with songs and tales and games galore we waited till the dawn.

'Cally' was the equivalent of the English colcannon.

At funerals, which usually proceeded from the deceased's home in those days, all the neighbouring young men gathered in some field out of sight of the house of mourning. There, for 2 or 3 strenuous hours, they indulged in athletic feats: jumping, weight throwing and weightlifting, long and high jumping, wrestling, etc. There was a friendly rivalry between opposing townlands and it was here that records were made or broken. Regular athletic or sports meetings were out of bounds in some areas as some landlords did not want land being cut up and trampled unduly by young men, whom they described as 'skylarking vagabonds'.

11

BEFORE THE FAMINE

When the English writer and farming expert Arthur Young toured Ireland 200 years ago, he was very critical of the wasteful farming methods he found there. Of course, he should have directed his fire more at the landlord class, who were mainly responsible. If a tenant tried to improve his farm or farm buildings, the landlord increased his rent and could evict him whenever he pleased.

One of the few things that pleased Arthur Young was the view of Lough Key from the Rock of Doon in North Roscommon. He classed it as the grandest scenery he had beheld in any part of the world. He appreciated the view all the more as he had been passing through plain uninteresting countryside when the view of Lough Key, with its wooded islands and their historic ruins, burst into view. For a similar reason, a traveller going through south-west Sligo between Tubbercurry and Ballina might feel enraptured when the view of Lough Talt comes into view.

Before coming to the lake from either direction, the visitor passes through the plain featureless foothills of the Ox Mountains, described by a geologist who toured the area as uninteresting hills of gneiss and schist. Close to the lake lies the lonely glen of Glanavoo. The holy well there, known as St Attracta's Well, was a popular place of pilgrimage in former times. At the north-western end of the lake a high, well-built stone wall encloses 13,000 acres of rough mountainside.

I had mistakenly taken this wall to be a boundary fence for one of the deer parks – which were so common as part of a landlord's estate in times gone by – until I learned that the wall and the ground enclosed by it were part of a land project initiated in 1839 by the Irish Waste Land Improvement Society. While the scheme was not over-ambitious, it was at least a beginning. Among its weak points, it was slanted more towards the benefit of its shareholders than to the slaving occupants of the land; it still offered no security of tenure to the tenants. The society in its preamble described its objectives as the provision of a liberal profit for the shareholders, as well as providing employment to the 'industrious and necessitous peasantry'.

In 1839, the society bought a bankrupt landlord's estate at Gleneask, near Lough Talt in County Sligo. This landlord had impoverished the tenants, as well as himself, with rent increases. This short-sighted policy had backfired on him so much that the society bought it cheaply. The society, in leasing this land, stipulated that no lease should run beyond the life of a tenant. This in itself was a disincentive to the tenant to improve his holding.

No lease was issued to the tenant with less than 20 Irish acres. Those with less than 20 acres were classed as tenants-at-will, meaning they had no claim on their holdings beyond day-to-day occupation. This maintained a high percentage of the tenants, over forty families in all, at the level of peons or squatters. Main drains were to be constructed at the society's expense, while the tenants were to make cross drains and surface drains. Thirty miles of roads were built by the society.

New houses were built to replace the houses of the tenants, which were described as being, with a few exceptions, 'badly built, damp, and wretched'. The society undertook to build cottages 30 feet long, 12–14 feet wide and 8–10 feet high, of stone or brick, with roofs of slate or thatch, at a cost to the tenants of £20 for each house.

Each holder was to have one or more cows, with an expected return of between 75 and 112lb of butter annually. This butter was expected to fetch 8*d* per pound in the Sligo butter market. If sold in the more convenient Swinford butter market, the price averaged ½*d* per pound less, and at that time every ½*d* counted.

The people's main food was potatoes and buttermilk. Labourers working for the society were paid 10*d* without food or 8*d* per day if a meal was provided. This was the summer rate for a 12-hour day; 2*d* per day less was paid for a 9-hour day in winter.

The society placed an emphasis on livestock rearing in preference to increased tillage. They claimed that increased livestock rearing would mean more fodder production and eventually more farmyard manure to enrich the land. Only a low percentage of the land could be classed as arable.

Some of the cottages were roofed with slate quarried in nearby Mount Taafe. However, the slate deposits were too inaccessible to encourage worthwhile production.

The Waste Land Improvement Society bought a second impoverished landlord's estate at Ballinakill in north Connemara around the same time as their purchase of the Gleneask estate. They proceeded to develop both estates along similar lines. Unfortunately, when they felt that they were making headway to the mutual benefit of their tenants and shareholders, the Great Famine of 1847 struck with full force. It resulted in two thirds of the society's tenants ending up in famine graves or aboard emigrant ships and the collapse of the Land Improvement Schemes.

To make matters worse, the tenants had grown more potatoes than usual. When the potato blight struck, it wiped out their promising potato crop in a few days.

The summer of 1847 was the wettest in living memory and with the stalks blighted, the tubers, in the words of a local man, 'stood no stagger', but rotted steadily in the sodden heavy clay. There had been local outbreaks of potato blight in 1845 and 1846, but with the continuous rain in 1847, the outbreak was nationwide.

There were warnings sounded by farming experts and public bodies in 1845 and 1846, but the government of the day callously ignored all of them.

12

Mountain Dew

Nor th and East Mayo, in common with other parts of Ireland where the distillation of poteen or illicit whiskey was routine, had their legendary characters famed for the good quality of their product or their resourcefulness in thwarting or evading the law.

Over 100 years ago, one of the best-known poteen makers in Mayo was a man known as 'Red' Owen Judge. He lived on a slope of the Ox Mountains, a few miles from Foxford. One day he set out for Foxford with a donkey carrying two creels of turf for sale. The creels were wickerwork or woven rod baskets suspended across the donkey's back. Under the turf in one creel was a gallon jar of poteen. Owen Judge heard that a new police sergeant (RIC) had been appointed to Foxford and he was anxious to sell as much poteen as possible before making his acquaintance. He had learned from another home brew expert in Sligo that the new sergeant was a good judge of a right drop and came down more heavily on those making bad stuff. As he came within a half mile of Foxford, he met the sergeant walking along leisurely.

The sergeant, of course, had found a description of Owen and others of the same profession in the barracks, so he guessed he had the right man for an interview. He casually held up Owen, and after a few words about the quality and price of the turf, he lifted a few sods and found the jar.

Owen betrayed no dismay, but asked him if he was the new sergeant. When the sergeant answered that he was, Owen told him that the jar contained a special good drop that he had been on his way to give to him because, said Owen, 'I heard a man from your last station in Sligo say that you were a good judge of real good stuff.'

After some consideration, the sergeant said, 'Well, in that case, carry on to Foxford and call to my house and leave the turf there as well as the jar. There is another jar there and cover the two jars well with the turf. Tell my wife I sent you, and God help you if your stuff is not as good as what is in the other jar,' added the sergeant with a smile.

Owen continued his journey to Foxford and went at once to the sergeant's house. He told the sergeant's wife that he was in a hurry and to hand him out the jar that was in the turf shed. 'Your husband is expecting a call this evening from the DI (District Inspector) and he does not like to have any poteen lying around when that man calls. I do not blame him for that,' added Owen, 'as the same DI would smell poteen a mile away.'

The sergeant's wife handed out the jar and Owen lost no time in taking it to the other end of the town and selling it along with his own jar. Knowing that the sergeant was trying night and day to get him, Owen had to lie low and be more vigilant than ever.

For a year or more, he made his whiskey in remote hideouts and got other people, who were not suspect, to sell it for him. After a year of caution, Owen decided to take a chance and run a round at home on Christmas Eve. When he got his plant set up and everything humming, he strolled out to his lookout spot. He had a good pair of field glasses, brought with him from England in his youth. When he focused his glasses on the road to Foxford, he was horrified to see the sergeant and two comrades less than a mile away, on foot and heading in his direction. He rushed indoors and dragged the still, worm, cooler, etc., into the bedroom. He then took the large fire and brought some of it into each of the two neighbours' houses on either side of his own. Hastily disrobing, he got into the hag bed, as most kitchen beds were then called.

He told his wife to call in the children and say he had just died. She did that and then she called in the woman next door to assist. She was called Mrs Judge and was a professional crier.

Criers were women who attended all wakes and funerals and cried and lamented, chanted the praises of the deceased and clapped their hands in paroxysms of grief. In many instances, criers did not know (nor care) who the deceased was. The sergeant and his men arrived just as the two women, having hung a set of white curtains outside the bed and placed a lighted candle on a chair beside it, were getting into their stride crying. Owen's children were crying too as they really believed that their father had died. When Owen's wife, between sobs, told the sergeant of his demise, he turned to his men and ordered a retreat, saying under his breath, 'Too bad he did not do this a year ago.' Some days later, the sergeant learned the true story. He at once applied for a transfer, stating that he felt the poteen menace was well under control in his area.

Another noted distiller who flourished in the same area a generation later was known as the Legger. He earned the title thanks to his prowess escaping on foot from his pursuers whenever they tried to surprise him at his distillery. His would-be captors guessed his identity from his long legs and massive strides, but could never get close enough to positively identify him. Finding himself under extra surveillance and with no income in sight, he wrote a brief note to the sergeant in Foxford, ostensibly as a tip-off. The note stated that the Legger would be taking a donkey cart load of turf to Foxford the next Saturday morning and that he would have a 2-gallon jar of poteen hidden in the turf. Delighted with the tip, the sergeant met the Legger on the outskirts of the town and told him he just then wanted a load of turf. When he asked what the price would be, the Legger said it was five shillings.

The sergeant felt that in the circumstances it was worth the price, so he told the Legger to take it around to his place and he would show him where to dump it. The Legger innocently asked him would the next load suit, as he had another customer waiting for turf. 'No,' said the sergeant, 'and here is your five shillings and get a move on. I can't be waiting all day.'

The Legger took the load around and emptied it under the vigilant eye of the sergeant, who found that he had got the nicest turf 'from Pollagh Bog to Knockfadda', to quote the Legger's own words.

I can remember an old woman of 80 from Killasser parish telling of the adventures of her father in the poteen-making industry.

'My father, grandfather and great-grandfather all had the name of making first-class whiskey. If a round did not turn out good as they expected, they would dump it rather than give their stuff a bad name. On one occasion, my father got an order for two gallons from the parish priest in Kiltimagh.

'We had a young half-trained horse at the time. I was a young schoolgirl, but being the oldest of the family, my father took me with him, partly to help with the horse and partly to attract less notice to our real business. He put the jar of whiskey in the cart and put a bag of hay over it. He told me to sit on the box and keep a tight hold of the horse's reins. He took a short hold of the horse's bridle and walked by his head all the way to Kiltimagh, 11 or 12 miles away.

'When we got to Kiltimagh, we found it was fair day there. When our horse saw all the cattle on the street, he began to prance and back away from them. The police barracks at that time was close by and the sergeant was standing outside.

'When he saw our trouble, he walked over and spoke to the horse and patted him. He then took a hold of the horse's bridle on the opposite side to my father. In that way, the horse gave no more trouble.

'When we got to the parish priest's gate, the sergeant turned back, giving me a slow wink as he did so. I heard afterwards that he was one of those who attended small parties in the priest's house sometimes. I have no doubt that he guessed who we were and had a good idea of our reason for going to the parish priest's house.

'My father always believed in leaving a drop outside for the good people (fairies) any night that he made a round. Any night he forgot this, he regretted it as that round would go against him. He always made sure to put the *braon broghach* (ugly drop) aside by itself to use as a rub for rheumatism, and a good cure it always was. Many a time it was a help to myself.'

The *braon broghach*, pronounced 'breen broagh', was the first two cupfuls of the round that came from the still. As its name implies, it tasted bitter, but it had its commercial value as a liniment.

In Feudal Days

During the famine years of 1845–49, many Mayo landlords, finding further evictions unprofitable and further increases in rack-rents impossible, initiated instead a system of forced labour. Tenants were forced to report to their landlord and work gratuitously according to the size of their rents: cultivating and reclaiming 'His Honour's' lands, levelling buildings and garden walls of evicted tenants and carrying out other useful works. Their reward was one meal daily for a working day of 12 hours.

One landlord in Killasser parish solved the problem of feeding his workers by driving out to them in his horse and cart with a tub of stirabout (Indian meal porridge). His son was heckled about it in later times at an election meeting in Swinford.

Years ago, I heard an old man from Carracastle parish who told me that his grandfather worked for a similar reward for his landlord, Thomas Phillips of Cloonmore. As the potato famine eased, the Cloonmore landlord changed the meal of porridge to a ration of potatoes, which the workers roasted in an open fire. This was termed a 'caste' of potatoes. As times improved and herrings got cheaper, a cooked salty herring wrapped in a cabbage leaf was occasionally sent out to each worker in addition to his potato caste. At Hagfield House nearby, dinner was served to the workers in the yard on a shovel.

On one occasion the Cloonmore slaves were busy digging out their landlord's potatoes alongside the Carracastle–Doocastle road. Around noon, a petty landlord, Joe Mór McDonnell of

Doocastle, emerged from the Big House, leading an old nag, after an all-night party with their landlord. Incidentally, Joe never referred to his residence as 'Doocastle', which is the common name for the region. Joe passed himself off as the owner of 'Doo Castle'.

Joe Mór complained to the starving workers that 'Tomeen' Phillips's geese were tough as leather and that after drinking four bottles of his wine and four of his whiskey; he was still going home sober.

Joe Mór McDonnell (Big Joe) was an impecunious Catholic squire from Doocastle, a remote border region between counties Mayo and Sligo. He was one of the most colourful Irish Members of Parliament and once attempted to smuggle his bagpipes into the Commons chamber. He was a member of the Repeal Association, Daniel O'Connell's political party.

A spendthrift, a gambler, a sportsman, a politician and a bankrupt, he was of colossal stature, with handsome, jovial features, and was remembered as the last of the old type of Irish county gentleman. Although his career in the Commons was short, his engagement with Irish political life was extensive, and he was never far from controversy.

He was known all over Mayo as the 'Doocastle Sunday Man', not due to his religious fervour but because Sunday was the only day of the week when he could claim immunity from arrest by his creditors if he left his own grounds. Joe's other claim to fame rested on his great size and phenomenal appetite. He sat as an MP for Mayo in the House of Commons after he was victorious over George Henry Moore of Moorehall with the aid of Archbishop McHale and the clergy in the famous 1847 election. Moore had enlightened national views and treated his famine-stricken tenants with more humanity than any other landlord in Mayo.

Joe Mór's term in the Commons was short as he was ousted by Moore the following year. During the 1848 election, it became known that he was not averse to a good meat dinner on Fridays and he was severely heckled about this at a meeting in Foxford.

Joe stood up as the heckling began and he took a letter from his pocket. He then asked if anybody in the audience could understand Italian. When he got the expected negative, he took the letter, waved it aloft, and offered a bet of £20 that it was in the handwriting of Pope Pius IX. He offered the money to anyone who could prove otherwise. Their wits dulled by famine and oppression, many believed the huge fraud. In offering a bet of £20, he was on safe ground as his listeners probably did not have £20 between them (and neither did Joe).

Then he read out the missive in his hand:

> My dear Joe, I am glad to hear that you are carrying on the fight for the ould faith in County Mayo. As a mark of my appreciation for your zeal and hard work, you are not to fast or abstain until the campaign is over.
> Yours truly, Pius IX.

In 1847, the opposition leader in the House of Commons, Lord Bentinck, sponsored a motion to allot £18 million for famine relief work in Ireland. Fearing another election, Joe Mór and another Mayo MP, Dillon Browne of Glencorrib, voted with the government and helped to defeat the motion. At the time, some of McDonnell's neighbours were dying on their way to Swinford workhouse.

Others were dying from surfeits of spawned salmon or trout, the toxic effects of which they were unable to withstand in their run-down condition. As the rivers and fish belonged to the landlords, this was a hush-hush matter. It should be noted that Gavan Duffy in his memoirs referred to Dillon Browne as 'the worst type of an Irish place hunter'.

By all accounts, Joe wasn't far behind him. He had at least one poem or 'planxty' composed in his honour, as was the custom in those days for people of the upper classes. It was hard to tell at times if the 'poem' was an act of flattery or a satire, as the composer always used exaggerated and colourful phrases. Such recitations were paraded before the public at weddings, wakes and all sorts of public meetings.

Three verses survive of this poem for Joe Mór:

> Long life to Your Honour,
> Joe Mór Myles McDonnell

Of far-famed Doo Castle in the County Mayo!
In a title of honour
You're the bright Star of Connacht
And in th' Irish character your name is Joe Mór.

You are the repaler
That never desaved us
You stood for oul' Erin abroad and at home.
In the sixth Verse or Chapter
'Twill be written hereafter
That you were the true member for the County Mayo.

At the door of Doo Castle
He vaults to his saddle
And away with him coursing and sporting go leor.
In wining or fighting
In speeching or writing
He bears off the palm for the County Mayo.

Other landlords were the subject or indeed the object of such poems. Sometimes it was wiser not to sing or recite such works in the vicinity of the landlord or any of his friends.

One of the most influential landlord families in East Mayo in those days were the Ormsbys of Ballinamore.* Thomas Ormsby sat on the jury that sent Fighting Fitzgerald to the gallows in 1796.

Three years later, he filled a similar role when Fr Conroy, the patriot priest of Addergoole, was sentenced to death in Castlebar. Over the lean post-famine years, his son, Black Anthony Ormsby, ruled in Ballinamore with the traditional severity of his ancestors towards his tenants. Yet he found one tenant pliable enough to compose a lengthy poem in praise of Ballinamore and its landlord. Despite the poet's lavish praise, only one line of the poem pleased Ormsby: 'I'm sure 'tis as strong as the temple of Rome.'

Another poem, 'The Whiskers of Ballinamore', was not so complimentary. It tells of a rent collection day in Ballinamore when Black Anthony ordered three tenants from his presence because they had grown whiskers, which he thought they had done in imitation of his own flowing black beard. He ordered:

> Get off those whiskers and that without delay,
> Or fifteen shillings yearly, with your rent you all must pay.

As refusal meant eviction, the tenants complied with his demand. In the opening lines, the poet sang,

> In the Parish of Killedan in the County of Mayo,
> There dwells a cruel landlord whose name I'll let you know.
> There rules a cruel landlord whose tenants suffer sore,
> And they call him Tony Ormsby, the Lord of Ballinamore.

Having sent all landlords to warm regions, the poet concludes:

> Now all you weary bachelors and rambling boys take care,
> If you happen to be tempted a whisker for to wear.
> Be wary of your landlord now and for evermore,
> Or else he might mistreat you like the Boy from Ballinamore.

*The Ormsbys' arrival in Ballinamore can be dated back to the aftermath of the Cromwellian wars and the arrival in the area of John Ormsby, an adventurer and an officer in Cromwell's army in 1651. He first purchased some land that had been seized from the previous owners and in the 1670s was granted the Ballinamore estate by royal patent. For well over 250 years, the Ormsbys of Ballinamore were one of the biggest landowning families in County Mayo. 'Black' Anthony Ormsby was recorded as owning almost 4,500 acres in 1876 – 200 years after his ancestor, John Ormsby, had founded the estate. But that was the heyday of the Ascendancy classes in Ireland and thereafter the family fortunes were to decline. All of the Ormsbys' property, with the exception of the 'Big House' and its immediate surrounds, had passed out of their ownership before the foundation of the Irish Free State. The house and grounds were bought by an order of nuns in 1938 and that marked the end of the Ormsbys of Ballinamore.

14

ULTACHS

I n my youth, I often heard the name 'Ultach' added to some people's names to distinguish them from others with similar surnames. I still hear this title applied, but not so frequently. On inquiring about the reason, I found that the Ultachs, meaning Ulster people, were descendants of the victims of Protestant bigotry and persecution who had to flee from Ulster, in some cases as far back as 1793. Around that time, a secret Protestant society was formed in north-east Ulster with the avowed object of banishing all Catholics to 'Hell or to Connacht', a statement which was a revival of Oliver Cromwell's proclamation over 150 years earlier. This secret society, which carried out acts of murder, arson and intimidation at daybreak, were named the 'Peep O' Day Boys'.

This society, after changing its name in 1795 to the Orange Society, earned and is still earning worldwide notoriety as the ultimate in religious bigotry and intolerance. In 1795, a convention of Ulster magistrates and lawmakers, presided over by Lord Gosford, Governor of Armagh, condemned the Orange Society as a 'lawless banditti guilty of dreadful murders and destruction of property'. All but one member of this convention were Protestants. Despite this, the religious persecution continued unabated.

Catholics who got the customary 12 hours' notice to get out were in one respect the lucky ones, as many were shot out and burned out (to quote an Orange Society report) without warning.

A society known as the Defenders sprang up to defend Catholic property, but with obsolete arms they had little hope of turning the tables on their well-armed opponents.

Much persecution came from County Armagh. Often those people who fled had to gather their livestock, poultry and other belongings and head for Connacht in the depths of winter. The journey to West Connacht sometimes lasted up to eight weeks, depending on weather conditions and the assistance or opposition they encountered on the way. Luckily for fleeing Catholics, they came at a time when Mayo landlords were looking for tenants, as they had many vacant holdings on their lands.

Emigration, chiefly to the United States and Canada, was getting into full swing and whole families were leaving Mayo every week. Many more holdings were vacant through the wholesale eviction policy of the more tyrannical of the landlords. The Ultachs brought advanced farming ideas with them to Connacht.

One of my informants said that even when it came to catching a salmon, snaring a trout or hare or making a good drop of mountain dew, they were hard to beat. One man of Ultach ancestry told me that he fully believed that his grandfather made the best *poitín* in Ireland.

He pointed to a small moss-covered ruin between 50 and 100 yards from his dwelling house and said, 'My grandfather was born and reared there.'

'Some time,' he continued, 'after my grandfather's parents died and his sisters had gone to America, he felt it was time to think of getting married. He decided to make a run of *poitín* as a first step. When he had all ready for firing, he got two neighbours to help him. He was getting a good return.

'He had very few bottles in hand, so he had almost every spare vessel in the house filled with *poitín*. Sometime after midnight, they all seemed to get weak with hunger and taking sips of the whiskey only made them worse, so my grandfather said he would cook something to eat. Two or three days before, a good calf belonging to one of his neighbours broke a leg and had to be killed and salted.

'The owner sent in a large lump of veal to my grandfather. In those days, if a neighbour had only one potato, he would share it with another one if he was in need of it. Today, they would hardly give you the *cuasán*.' (The *cuasán* was a vacant space or vacuum at the core of the potato, sometimes equal to the size of a large marble. It seems something was lacking in the growth and formation of the potato which retarded the completion of its growth. I have not seen a *cuasán* (pronounced 'coosaun') in a potato over the past fifty years. Possibly the use of more fertilizers has helped the potato to close this gap. In those days, most of the heifer calves were sold to butchers for killing to keep down the cattle population.)

My informant continued: 'My grandfather put the veal in a small pot or skillet and hung it over the fire but it seems he put the veal in the wrong pot. He had the first dash of *poitín*, called the *braon broghach* (ugly drop) in one pot. It was as inflammable as paraffin oil.

'Before they noticed anything, the chimney was blazing and then the thatch. My grandfather had barely enough time to grab his best clothes and whatever money was in the house and get out before the house all went up on fire. When the neighbours gathered the next day to thatch the house again, my grandfather said he would wait a day or two.

'He felt that the house was too near the old fairy fort at the back and he never seemed to have much luck in it. He went to a wise woman who lived above the town of Swinford, Bid Heaney. When she came, she pointed out this spot instead for building the house on. My grandfather did as she told him and found he had better luck after that.'

ι

15

OLD CHARMS
AND CUSTOMS

Superstitious and semi-superstitious customs and charms were a significant feature of rural life in Ireland up to and during the famine years. Whole villages were wiped out by the famine or by the succeeding mass evictions by rack-renting land-lords and many old traditions disappeared forever. But some of the old customs lingered on, even until our own time.

A charm or cure that seemed to be popular in South Mayo until a couple of generations ago was Crean's Blood. This meant blood belonging to anybody by the name of Crean, locally pronounced 'Creheen'.

It was believed that a few drops were an infallible cure for lung or chest ailments if the blood was diluted with hot water and the vapour inhaled by the affected person. I can recall being told by an old man of a trip made by him to an old woman of the Crean clan for a cure for his grandmother, who was 'caught up in the chest'.

The old woman with the Crean surname simply tied her index finger at two points near the tip and base, made a small gash on her finger between the two points and gave him the required blood. The man's grandmother said she felt a big improvement after having tried the remedy. The blood donor took no cash in payment but accepted 2oz of tobacco and a noggin of whiskey as a gift.

I remember in my younger days listening to an old man, Ned Flanagan, telling of a trip he once made to the far end of Kilmovee parish on behalf of his young wife, who got a dust or a hayseed in her eye while haymaking. His trip was to an old woman who possessed cure for disorders of the eyes.

According to Ned Flanagan, this old woman, on hearing his story, got a saucer of spring water, made the sign of the cross over it and said what he believed to be a prayer in a low voice. She then called Ned over and showed him the cause of his wife's trouble: a small hayseed which had begun to sprout. Having left a small bottle of whiskey as a present for the old woman, Ned set out on the 16-mile walk to his home.

On his arrival, his wife informed him that she felt instant relief in the affected eye at around three o'clock in the afternoon, which was around the time Ned had been shown the hayseed floating in the saucer of water.

To cure boils, carbuncles or external blemishes, bathing in water at a point where three parishes met (or, better still, four parishes) was recommended.

The thread to cure sprains was confined to, and handed down in, certain families. If an old man or woman possessing the sprain thread had no family or if all his family had emigrated, the thread was handed down to a niece, nephew or some other close relation. When any sufferer had occasion to send for the sprain thread, the messenger was instructed to go 'around the road', as taking a short-cut through fields was believed to lessen the speedy efficacy of the charm.

If anybody was lucky enough to collect the dropping seeds of the royal fern (*Raithneach na Rí*), he was said in olden times to have a charm worth his weight in gold. One snag was that the seeds had to be collected at midnight on St John's Eve, a date to which a lot of old beliefs were linked. May Day (1 May) and Samhain Eve, the eve of 1 November, were also favourite dates for old ideas and customs.

An object of mixed fear and veneration in Kilcummin churchyard in North Mayo was the *Leac Cuimín* or Cuimín's flagstone. St Cuimín was said to have been washed ashore as an infant in a frail boat and found and adopted by a local man named Maughan. Cuimín adopted a religious hermit's life when he grew up and built his little church, which gave the name Kilcummin to the spot. On his deathbed, he is said to have bequeathed the flagstone to be placed over his grave to the Maughan family, together with the power to use the stone for cursing slanderers and evil-doers.

If anybody for miles around felt badly wronged by a neighbour, he had first to fast for fifteen days and then employ the Maughan in charge of the *Leac Cuimín* to turn it over if he wanted to avail of the powers of the *leac* to get even with the one he felt had wronged him. A walk around St Cuimín's Well nearby before the curse functionary was also included in the rituals. A Maughan always turned the stone and intoned the curse for a stiff fee.

In the course of time, the Loughneys (another local sept that had intermarried with the Maughans) claimed a right to use the stone, which was becoming a lucrative possession. Feuds and faction fights ensued, especially on the annual pattern day in Kilcumnin, and this went on for generations.

In the 1830s, the son of a local parson named Waldron decided that the stone was bringing the district into disrepute because of all the fights and squabbles of which it was now the centrepiece. He took a sledge hammer at night and broke the stone into fragments. This resulted in a rush to collect the fragments to use them for the same purposes as the original stone – to curse one's enemies. The situation became so bad that Dean Lyons, then administrator of Ballina Cathedral, had the fragments of the stone collected and built into the masonry of the new cathedral, where they have remained since.

16

A Tale of
Barnalyra Wood

A film director on the lookout for a suitable setting for an eerie film would probably regard Barnalyra, about 5 miles south-east of Swinford, County Mayo, as an ideal location.

The extensive woods that once covered the bleak hills and steep gorges have practically disappeared. Most of the trees remaining are stunted, twisted or commercially useless specimens, which resemble brooding spectral sentinels guarding a shady past and adding to the loneliness of the locality. It is small wonder, then, that Barnalyra can boast a unique ghost of its own with the unusual name of the *Beicheadán*.

A couple of centuries ago, according to local legend, a poor cottier and his wife lived in a clearing in Barnalyra Wood, along the road, which at the time was the main road from Sligo to Galway.

In later times, this road was the route used by the Bianconi mail coaches travelling from Sligo to Galway. The cottier and his wife had a daughter, an only child who grew up to be a remarkably handsome girl and was acclaimed the belle at every local *céilí* and crossroads gathering. The man and his wife felt that with such a beautiful daughter and no money for her dowry they had been cruelly slighted by Providence.

They became obsessed with the notion that owing to their poverty, she would eventually marry some local herd- or gamekeeper and spend her life in poverty and drudgery.

One summer evening, a passing stranger called and asked for a meal and, if possible, a bed for the night, promising to pay well.

He said he had been at sea for some years, and having left his ship at Sligo, he hoped to visit his aged parents at the southern end of County Mayo.

The couple gladly agreed to his request. Saying that he felt tired and footsore, the sailor retired to the little room pointed out to him by his hostess. On peeping into the room through a chink in the door sometime later, the cottier saw his visitor counting a neat pile of golden coins. He and his wife decided that this was a golden opportunity to provide their daughter with a dowry. They first sent the daughter to stay overnight with an aunt who lived a mile distant. When night fell, they stealthily entered their visitor's bedroom and took his life.

Then they buried his body in the nearby wood, they buried his head separately in the nearby Curragh Bui bog to ensure that the body could not be identified. After a few days had elapsed, stories began to circulate about a headless man being seen rushing along the road by Barnalyra Wood after nightfall. Many people scoffed at the tale but gradually even the most incredulous of the local people admitted having seen the headless ghost, which in time they named the *Beicheadán* (the Screamer). The drivers of the Bianconi mail coaches plying between Sligo and Galway always strove to be clear of Barnalyra Wood before nightfall, once the story of the *Beicheadán* gained more publicity.

According to the legend, the cottier and his wife met untimely deaths. The cottier was killed by a tree he was felling and his wife's body was found in the stream that flows parallel to the road through the wood after a flood one year later. She told the terrible secret of the sailor's murder to her daughter sometime before her death. Her daughter lost her reason and pined away and died a short time after her mother.

The legend of the *Beicheadán* lingered on until comparatively recent times. In 1924, a very wet summer created a fuel scarcity and this, coupled with the unsettled state of the country, resulted in Barnalyra Wood almost disappearing in a few months. People within a 10-mile radius of Barnalyra flocked to the wood, ostensibly for firewood, but as most of the timber was first-class larch, beech and pine, a very small fraction was used for firewood.

17

The Lad from Inishkea

N orth and South Inishkea islands, off the West Mayo coast, were a noted nursery for a hardier than average type of west of Ireland manhood.

This hardiness sprang from a harsh and unrelenting struggle for survival with primitive boats and equipment in stormy seas. The rocky, inhospitable soil of the islands and the long row to the mainland helped to add to the islanders' unceasing struggles and worries. The inhabitants of the two islands were taken to the mainland and allotted holdings of land by the Irish Land Commission about four decades ago.

Prior to their migration, the people on the neighbouring mainland liked to indulge in jokes reflecting the gullibility and innocence of the islanders.

One such story was told of a young lad from Inishkea who came to visit relatives in the mainland parish of Ballycroy. In those relatives' house, he saw a round earthenware jar minus the handle. On questioning his host about the jar, the lad from Inishkea was told that the jar was a mare's egg, and that if it were placed on a hob or some warm spot by the fire and turned regularly, a young foal would emerge after eleven months.

When leaving for home, the young lad was presented with the jar by his host as a memento of his visit. The jar, bound with a straw rope, was placed on his back and he left in high spirits for Inishkea. The day being warm and the journey to the ferry for Inishkea a lengthy one, the young visitor soon grew tired and sat down to rest on top of a steep hill. As he sat down, the jar slipped out of the straw rope and rolled rapidly down the hillside. It crashed into a large rock and broke into fragments.

Immediately, a hare resting on the other side of the rock took flight at top speed, with the lad from Inishkea watching with admiration, as no hares exist on Inishkea. Concluding that the hare was the horse foal released from the mare's egg by the crash, he exclaimed in Irish, '*M'anam o'n diabhal*, when he is a two-year-old, the devil out of Hell won't catch him!'

Another tall tale about a lad from Inishkea, which also involves a hare, was one of my grandfather's special yarns. As I am not committing myself to say how much of the story is to be believed, I will tell it in his own words.

'In my young days,' said my grandfather, 'I once hired a *spailpín fánach* who called on me in search of work. He was a native of Inishkea. He was a fine, supple, lively lad, every footstep about 2 yards long when walking. His name was Manus Lavelle.

'One summer evening, I showed him a steep sandpit with a narrow sloping entrance. I told him that I wanted the sheep and lambs flocked into the sandpit the next morning, in order to pick out the fattest lambs to take to the fair of Claremorris the following day.

'The lad was out in good time next morning and after a quick breakfast went off to round up the sheep, while I waited to milk the cows before going to his assistance. When I got to the sandpit, I found he had the sheep already gathered and among them a large, panting hare.

"Oh Manus," I exclaimed, "you have a hare along with the sheep."

"Arrah," Manus replied coolly. "Is that what you call him? Well, believe me, that little devil gave me more trouble than all the rest!"'

The yarn of the mare's egg, still popular in Ballycroy, must be a very old one as it was related by Maxwell in his *Wild Sports of the West*, written nearly 180 years ago.

18

From Matriarchs to Piteógs

Listening to a lively debate on the subject of Women's Liberation or 'Lib' helped to take my memory back to a *seanchaí* or storyteller of my early youth who specialised in debates on the same subject. He was known to one and all as 'Michael the Yank'. He had been a schoolteacher for a few years until, in his own words, he fell out with the system and the customs of the time and getting paid only once a quarter. He then 'lit out for the Land of the Almighty Dollar'.

On his return, he often stopped at our home when coming back from the town.

He would regale us with old local stories and tales of his experiences in America. Since he regarded me as an attentive listener, he always took me a 'ha'porth' of sweets, which in those days meant thirty or forty bullseyes of the canned sweets type.

He could mix doleful stories with stories in a lighter vein. I can vividly remember one of his accounts about priest-hunting, murder and persecution in the Penal Days.

'Oh, well,' he would say, 'priests and people can both breathe more freely today and can enjoy a joke in its own time. I remember that when I was a lad, a young man from my mother's part of the country was ordained a priest. My mother took me with her when she called on his father to offer her congratulations. Now, the priest had a younger brother who was sitting beside his father at the fireside when we called. Unlike the new priest, this individual did not live up to the behaviour standards expected of him. My mother congratulated the old man and said it was a great privilege to have a priest in the family.

'The old man said it was indeed a great privilege and then added, "As a matter of fact, I'm thinking of making a priest out of that black devil over there!"'

On another occasion, when Michael the Yank called to our house, the burning topic of the day was the struggle for women's rights; chiefly the right to vote in Parliamentary elections.

The suffragettes, as the campaigners were called, could command a large degree of support, especially amongst the working classes. Launching into this topic, Michael was in his element. As he himself was a bachelor, he could judge the subject more objectively than most and being a voracious reader of up-to-date periodicals helped him to know what he was talking about. Or so he believed.

'There was a time in Irish society when women ruled the roost. Back then, under matriarchal laws the men had narrow corners.

'Some of them lived in terror of being picked by a queen or some other powerful lady to be one of her many husbands and of being snuffed out later by some other jealous husband. This often happened with the connivance of "Her Ladyship". In those days of indeterminate fatherhood, a man's nearest relatives were reckoned to be his sister's children!

'Gradually, as private property – a disturbing element, as always – crept into the reckoning, the monogamous or single marriage evolved to solve the problem.

'One writer in Ancient Greece, who deplored the introduction of the single marriage, wrote that brother will fight against brother and sisters' children will break the bonds of blood.

'It could indeed be that he was in the pay of some old "hairpins" who wanted the old system to continue. It's a fact that most of the history of the world was written down by historians under orders from their tyrant bosses. Otherwise, they might have to go looking for their heads! It was a long, uphill struggle for the men and even when they got on even terms, there was still an odd old queen, like the beehive queen, who could show who them the boss was.

'Our own Queen Maeve was no joke in this regard and wasn't there a queen in Britain who used to lead her conscripts against the Roman legions until her final defeat in AD 42?

'There was another old battle-axe who was responsible for the Battle of Clontarf. What we have been led to believe was a glorious struggle for freedom was really only the outcome of a family struggle.'

I do feel that Michael the Yank was on solid ground here: Brian Boru had married the mother of the Danish leader, Sitric, after getting shut out by his own brother, Mahon, the rightful heir to the High Kingship of Ireland.

At that time, as now, it was easy to stir up a family squabble. Of course, Brian did not carry a cross before his men into battle at Clontarf. Like William Tell's apple or Nero fiddling while Rome burned (a good 1,000 years before the fiddle was invented), those stories are fables.

You can add in the story about Patrick Sarsfield taking a handful of his blood at the Battle of Landen and saying, 'Oh that this was for Ireland.' Like others all around him, Sarsfield was fighting for the preservation of his landed estates and of his standard of life; the notion of nationhood was still far away into the future.

To continue where Michael the Yank left off, I may add that the famine and Tithe War, as well as the Land War, produced their own quota of unsung heroines. Parnell's sister, Anna, who founded the Women's Land League and had to fight an uphill struggle against Church and state, as well as against her own brother, on behalf of the starving peasantry, deserves to be remembered. The advent of the twentieth century ushered in a period that Michael the Yank termed an armed truce between the sexes. 'I fear,' he once told me, 'that the men of Ireland are fast becoming a race of *piteógs*.'

In Michael's estimation, a *piteóg* is a degenerate type who insists on doing women's work and is constantly bowing to them, at least in a figurative sense. (*Piteóg* is an old Gaelic word that in modern English would be the equivalent of 'sissy'.)

The cold war situation in Ireland between progressive male and female elements in the early years of the twentieth century manifested itself in songs and poems of dubious literary merit.

I can recall a duet sung by ladies in praise of one of their gender who rejected the attentions of a hard-drinking Romeo with the words,

> There is an inn where you call in as I hear some people say,
> Where you tap and call and pay for all and go home at the break of day.

A composition from the other side tells of a young married man whose light of love turned out to be a scolding dame. The aggrieved young man went to his godfather for advice on the matter. The 'song' concluded with the words:

> Just get a little stick, do not get it very thick but just about the thickness
> of your thumb,
> And lay it on her back 'till her bones begin to crack,
> And 'tis then you'll get ease from her tongue, tongue, tongue.

A minor poet from Rathduff, near Balla, decided to add a further verse to add insult to injury, as it were. His contribution ran,

> I took my friend's advice and I went home to my wife,
> And I laid the timber on her back '*go trom*' (heavily),
> I beat her body round, made the holy hazel sound,
> And was then I got relief from her tongue, tongue, tongue,
> Oh, 'tis then I got ease form her tongue.

He got a pal of his, a reasonably good singer, to contribute the song with the added verse to a concert in Balla, where it nearly caused a riot. I do not intend to step in where angels fear to tread in the realms of Women's Lib and other organisations. Their questions and grievances are linked to many controversial side issues in the social, economic and political fields.

In temporal matters, production and distribution for unreasonably excessive profits are the true enemies of real charity and brother-hood. The old maxim that the value of any commodity should be determined by the necessary social labour involved in its production is a dead duck today. So the production of alcohol, drugs, arms and other lethal weapons of destruction goes on unabated.

FISHY STORIES

L iving in an area removed from the larger Irish lakes and rivers (with the exception of the River Moy), I was not conversant with many of the customs and taboos associated with inland fishing in Ireland. One of my earliest recollections is of being chased home by my elders when found fishing for perch in the River Moy on Whit Sunday. Two or three other youthful anglers shared my fate on that occasion.

I have never been able to discover the reason for why fishing is forbidden on Whit Sunday and yet it is, a ban which is still rigidly observed in parts of the West of Ireland.

Apart from fishing, boatmen in some parts will not go on the water alone on that day. Four small lakes, two on each side of the roads, lie close to each other midway between Swinford and Kikelly. They are located in rough unfenced commonage and border three townlands – Shammer, Tullinahoo and Cornaveagh.

Faction fights and quarrels were a regular occurrence in the days of old as each townland claimed the lakes and the surrounding com-monage – or tried to claim these rights. One of those lakes is called *Loch na mBreach Caoch* (the Lake of the Blind Tout).

On enquiring about the reason for the name of this lake, I was told that formerly the larger trout in this lake were blind in one eye and sometimes in both, and that occasionally trout so affected are still caught there. Re-stocking has possibly improved the quality of the fish there. Regardless of the legendary reasons, I believe that

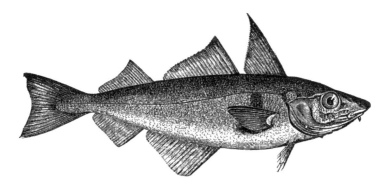

low PH or high concentrations of bog acid in the water may be a
contributory factor.

As regards the *Loch na mBreach Caoch* near Kilkelly, the old tale
held that many generations ago a local man went fishing on the
lake in question on Whit Sunday and caught a large trout, which he
landed with his gaff. Taking the trout which he had gaffed through
the eye, he put it in the scouring tub and covered it over until he had
time to prepare and cook his fish. Returning some hours later, he
found his trout gone, without a trace. Every trout he caught after that
was blind or had diseased eyes and he always threw them back in the
lake again.

Fifty years ago, a man was drowned while fishing for white trout
on Christmas Day on the picturesque Glenmurry River. An old man
from the same district told me that the man in question was the author
of his own misfortune because he had fished on Christmas Day.

No fish in Irish rivers or lakes is surrounded by so much mystery
and superstition as the eel. The legendary *Rí Eascóin* or king eels
who were supposed to lead their hosts downstream to their long-
hidden spawning grounds were regarded with superstitious dread.

When travelling downstream to spawn during the waning moon,
the eel shoals emit a half-hissing, half-whistling noise that the old
folk believed was the marshalling call of the *Rí Eascóin* as he led
his followers to the spawning grounds and eventual death in the
Sargasso Sea.

This sea has only recently been identified as the eels' spawning ground. A good many years ago, people living near the Yellow River in the Knock–Kiltimagh area heard the sound of a large shoal moving slowly downstream. As the Yellow River enters Cultibo Lake and emerges at the opposite end, this slowed down the movement of the eels and gave a local man time to send a message to two brothers that lived a mile downstream.

They were active poachers and owned a strong close-mesh eel net. They hastily strung their net across the river. When the shoal of fish hit the net, they swept right on, taking the net and its mooring ropes with them. The poachers said that they had little fishing luck afterwards and they resolved not to interfere with the *Rí Eascóin* or his plans again.

Near Dunmascreena Bridge, between Claremorris and Dunmore on the Mayo–Galway border, I witnessed an unusual type of eel fishing. Local people run a stout cotton thread longitudinally through a number of earthworms. They then roll the worms into a ball and drop them into the river at the end of a strong fishing line. This is done on a dark night when there is a 'rise' or flood during the waning harvest moon, when the eels are moving downstream during the first stage of their journey to their spawning grounds.

When the eel takes the bait, his teeth get caught in the soft cotton thread.

When the fisher feels a slight tug on the line he hauls up his eel without a struggle. Strangely, eels do not struggle in darkness. I saw one operator land twenty-four eels at the historic bridge of Duamascreena in this fashion about fifty years ago. He called this system of eel fishing 'bobbing'.

In the naked limestone belt that runs from Balla in County Mayo to the Burren in Clare, there are countless turloughs or winter lakes, which in many instances dry up in summer. Larger ones recede to pools no more than a few square yards in size called 'swallow holes'. Eels were caught in their thousands in the swallow holes as they dried up and were salted in tubs and discarded butter firkins in less opulent days.

The skin of an eel was regarded as an infallible cure for wrist sprain or *talach* when wrapped around the wrist. Skins of large eels were used as whangs or fuangs for threshing flails to join the *colapán* to the *buailtín* or beater stick. There is also the partly solved mystery of the dog eel, which was believed to evolve from the hair of a dog. I have often observed wriggling live hairs in ponds and wells, but can offer no opinion as to their origin or eventual fate.

Large-scale drainage of peat bogs and low ponds has, in the opinion of many anglers, hastened the decline in the numbers of the trout population.

The deepening and widening of streams and drains from virgin bogs and swamps ensure that high-colour floodwater builds up and spills over much faster than of old. This militates against the trout more than other types of fish.

I should, perhaps, add a few lines on the dying art of salmon poaching with candle and gaff. This was a dangerous exercise in the perpetual war between the prevention bailiffs and the poachers or illegal fishermen.

Clashes between the bailiffs and poachers occasionally had fatal results. Sometimes armed bailiffs found themselves overpowered. In salmon poaching, a 'candle' could be a canvas bag or a disused sheet or blanket, or any material that would absorb paraffin oil (kerosene) and burn well. This oil-soaked material wrapped around a light steel bar or pole – when ignited and held aloft – threw a powerful light over a wide area. The glare momentarily dazzled the spawn-sick salmon, which was gaffed by the alert fisherman before the salmon knew what was happening.

On more than one occasion, fishermen lost their lives by wading into deep holes or were dragged there by unusually large salmon. Encumbered by rubber waders or pigskin protective clothing, the poacher often found himself handicapped in the icy and frequently flooded waters. On a dark night, it was a colourful sight to see up to a dozen 'candles' blazing on a short stretch of river or adjacent rivers. Nowadays, the poacher drives in his car to a salmon ford, unrolls his net and silently gets his fish. His system may be safer and more efficient, but it is certainly not as glamourous as the way 'the brigands of the midnight fords' operated.

The candle and gaff technique was also used to a lesser extent to catch spawning trout. During the famine years, the smaller rivers and lakes in the West of Ireland were said be almost scoured clean of fish by every legal or illegal means that could be devised.

In a townland bordering the Trimogue River between Swinford and Kiltimagh (*Cnoc Breac*), after surfeits of spawned salmon and trout, a system called 'routing' was devised that almost cleaned out all the fish in small rivers. A large turf *cliabh* or basket was placed in a stream with the mouth facing upstream. Around the sides of the basket sods were placed to ensure that no fish escaped downstream.

Two operators with shovels went 40 or 50 yards upstream and began systematically plunging their shovels into the sides of the stream to frighten all fish into the *cliabh*. When they got to the basket, it was smartly lifted and the fish tipped put. I can remember seeing up to a dozen fish, mostly trout, in the *cliabh* after a rout. After one recent rout, I saw two youngsters who had been told of this system trying their luck. All they got was one sickly looking trout.

In the good old days when trout were more plentiful, I saw a system for snaring trout on the Dalton River, separating Knock and Kilcolman parishes. The brown trout in clear, shallow water have a habit of darting forward and then stopping dead for a few seconds.

The angler gets three or four long ribs of hair from a cow or horse's tail, preferably white or grey in colour to avoid detection by the trout. He plaits the ribs of hair for strength. He then ties a loop of the hair to a rod and drops one end of the loop into the water in the expected path of the trout. If the trout comes to rest in the loop, one flick of the fisherman's wrist is enough to send him several yards inland.

In conclusion, it may not be out of context to mention a poem written in 1880 by Edmund O'Byrne Gear, in which he draws comparisons between migrant fish and our own emigrants. Gear was a national teacher domiciled in Kiltimagh. He taught for some years in Cultibo (old school) in the heart of fishing and poaching territory. He could compose a reasonably good poem on almost any subject in a specified time for a bet; the bet usually taking the form, in his own words, of 'liquid nourishment'. Gear's love for convivial company led to him ending his days as a night-watchman for a timber importing firm at Liverpool docks. An old man from Slievehorn told me many years ago that he knew Gear in Liverpool.

On one occasion he said that Gear, after eating his lunch, sat down on a pile of timber and selected a clean, smooth board on which he began to write a poem dedicated to the overworked, underpaid Irish workers in Liverpool. A works manager, who was passing by, came over to Gear and smilingly admired his poem and handwriting. Remarking that Gear must have seen better days, he offered him a responsible office job. Gear sadly shook his head, saying, 'I have earned my fate and must abide the consequences.'

20

MIGRANTS AND EMIGRANTS

(A poem by Edmund O'Byrne Gear)

Last night I passed the bare, brown sweep of bog beside the Yellow River,
Where solitude and silence keep unquestioned reign and state forever.
And there I heard a plaintive cry, like 'caoiners' oe'r a fallen king,
And saw against the starlit sky, a wild goose flight its spearhead fling.
By some strange instinct surely led, their northern pathway swiftly taking
From Eire's fragrant shores they fled to where pale frozen wastes
are quaking.

Later, I crossed the salmon ford to reach Killedan's verdant valley,
And saw a glittering silver horde of young smolts through the water sally.
From many a willow-girdled pool through many a crooning
sandy shallow,
Like children glad released from school as the swiftly darting swallow
For Mother Nature sends her call to those, her children of the deep.
And fast through ford and foaming fall, their onward march they
faithful keep.

Today I came by Garryroe, as dawn's sweet radiance filled the land
And I saw a sad procession go, all destined for a foreign strand.
Boys in their early youth and prime; girls with their unspoilt
maiden charm,
Fated to pass by haunts of crime; God keep their simple souls from harm.
Solemn, I spoke to Michael Clarke, 'Thou art a wise, far-seeing man,
Make bright to me the seeming dark; is Eire placed 'neath Heaven's ban?'
'The wild goose leaves the sun-browned moor for frozen wastes and
arctic seas.

The salmon flees from waters pure to where the shark exacts his fees.
Upon our land hath Heaven's power its withering wrath
revengeful spent,
That thus our nation's youth and poor outcasts like Ishmael now are sent
To fields where foul weeds rankly grow; where vice contends with
nature's plan,
Where souls are chained to Earth below and Mammon sears the
heart of man?'
Said Michael, sad but undismayed, 'Deep have I delved in ancient lore,
My musings with the past have made day bright things seeming
dark before.
I've schooled myself in nature's laws; I know the ways of beasts and men,
But when think of God, I pause and am a simple child again.

There are three or four more verses to this poem, but so far I have failed to collect them. I recently discovered two lines of one of the missing verses in which Gear mentions the salmon that always returns, unlike the emigrant who rarely returns:

When Samhain's harvests safe are stored, the vaulting salmon will return,
And brigands of the midnight ford again their flaming torches burn.

Edmund O'Byrne Gear was a bachelor. However, he nourished a secret affection and admiration for a girl from 'the mountain' (Slievehorn) and composed a poem in her honour:

There are many maidens in Mayo, so bright and blithe and bonny,
But there's not one of all I know to equal Maggie Moloney.
Her home is where the wild winds blow, o'er banks and bleak land stony,
Yet, not a flower our gardens grow, can equal Maggie Moloney.

Gear wrote poems on social problems. His assessment of politicians and statesmen, whose aims were to 'delude the masses', showed an analytical judgement of political science well ahead of his time.

21

TALES OF A *SPAILPÍN*

A favourite *seanchaí* or storyteller in my locality was a *spailpín* or seasonal migratory worker. He was known as Tom Dick. His surname I have forgotten. A discreet, unassuming, well-spoken bachelor, he was a natural-born storyteller. In addition, he had been a good athlete in his youth but his shyness prevented him from attaining his full potential as an athlete.

His tales of the trials and troubles of Irish migratory workers were a mixture of humour and pathos. Over 100 years ago, most of the *spailpíns* from the west of Ireland had a fair knowledge of Gaelic and this was an advantage if they did not want the native English to know what they were talking about.

'The first year I went to England,' said Tom, 'I went with my father. The Shah of Persia was on a visit to England. Finding his country to be rich in oil, the British government invited him over. He was wined and dined in a big way. At the farewell party, the poor Shah got such an overdose of food and wine that he behaved undacently.' (His reported 'undacent' act was to get up from the table and attempt to relieve himself behind one of the dining room curtains.) When the Irish workers in England got to hear about this, you can be sure they added to the tale.

'Have you seen the Shah today?' was a favourite catchphrase whenever they met up. When some of them got sacked for this, they changed the phrase to Gaelic. '*An bhfaca tú an Shah inniu?*' became the greeting.

Years later, the Boer War was to provide a ready outlet for the *spailpíns'* wit and sarcasm. In the early years of this war, the conspicuous, over-decorated uniforms of the British officers, largely drawn from the ranks of the upper classes, made them sitting ducks for the Boer snipers. The Boers picked them off with monotonous regularity. After some time the British got wise to this and the uniforms were made less conspicuous. A favourite piece of doggerel among the *spailpíns* contained the following lines:

> Our dukes and earls, our nation's pearls,
> From dodging bullets, their necks are sore,
> It is no nigger who pulls the trigger,
> But a real sharpshooter; the Transvaal Boer.

'On one occasion,' said Tom, 'I walked into a big public house row between our *spailpíns* and a bunch of English navvies after this song was sung. I had only landed from Ireland the same morning and I had a big oatmeal cake with me that I had brought over from Ireland. Those oatmeal cakes were harder than the devil's horns. In the thick of the row was a big English navvy who was too good for any of our lads. I later learned that he was a trained boxer. Seeing him head in my direction, I backed off and swung my cake that was wrapped in a calico cloth. I managed to hit him on the side of the head.

'He went down for the count and a bit more. Seeing their hero down, the English navvies fled and we soon put a few miles between us and that town before night.

'A story often told by a member of our gang helped to start trouble a good few times. This story was about an English landlord's son who went to South Africa to fight the Boers. He first went to his tailor and ordered a special uniform that was to include a steel plate in the front of the jacket to protect his heart. He told the tailor to hurry things along as he was afraid that the war would be over before he had the honour of fighting for his country.

'Well, the tailor rushed the job so much that he forgot about the metal plate until he had the vest complete. As he still had the pants to tailor, he had the bright idea of inserting the plate in the seat of the pants.

'He had only inserted the plate and had padded it comfortably when the aristocrat rode up to collect it. He did not have time for a fitting but just grabbed his uniform and headed straight for the nearest seaport and on to the war front. In his very first skirmish, he and some of his companions were greeted by such a hail of bullets that they turned around and fled at top speed with heads up and tails down. A few bullets hopped off the steel plate but the wearer was otherwise unharmed. When they got a safe distance from the danger, he and his companions dismounted at a roadside alehouse to celebrate their escape.'

According to Tom, when the mail-clad warrior was called on to say a few words to mark the occasion, all he could think of was, 'God bless my old tailor, he knew where my heart was better than myself.'

'In our *spailpín* gang,' continued Tom, 'there was a young man who would surely have been a world-champion boxer if he got the training or the chances that boxers get nowadays. His name was Mick Carroll and he came from the Cleerhy district, near Kiltimagh. In those days, cockfighting was not unusual and meetings for this cruel sport were often held in quiet places. Mick Carroll owned a fighting cock and also a fighting terrier. Mick was as active as a circus acrobat and he could walk on his hands and perform cartwheels and spins as good as any circus performer.

'Whenever he attended a cockfight meeting, he would issue a challenge to fight any man, cock or dog on behalf of himself and his team. Another man in our group had been a schoolmaster who lost his job for hitting an inspector who had charged him with being drunk. We called this man "The Rhymer" because he was always composing rhymes and poems about somebody or other. He composed a rhyme about Mick Carroll, but I can only now remember a line or two:

> A health to Mickeen Carroll, he's a whopper you must know,
> His native place is Kiltimagh in the county of Mayo.

'I went back to school for two winters after spending the first two summers in England and so did some of my mates. There was no compulsory schooling in those days; you just went if your parents had nothing else for you to do. I think the master was glad when he finally saw the back of us.

'Before the railway came, we used to tramp to Ballina or Sligo to take the boat for England.

'One time, we were joined in Ballina by nearly 100 Achill men. They had walked nearly 80 miles and were as light on their feet as deer. They came over the mountains near Nephin through a pass called Mam A' Scardáin. All were Irish speakers.

'Once we were hurrying to Ballina around six o'clock in the morning when we found that the only watch we had amongst us had stopped. It was a big old-timer, about the size of a small clock. We all had to run for the last 4 or 5 miles, after walking more than 25 miles before that, and then found we had plenty of time to spare.

'I remember once getting on a train to Dublin and getting stuck near there. It was eight or nine o'clock before we got to the Broadstone Station. When we were leaving Claremorris, one of our gang asked for a ticket to the "broad flag". He could not think of the right name for the place we were going to get off at.

'At the Broadstone, we were directed to a small hotel in the locality. We were informed that they were all booked up, but they had a big back kitchen and a couple of old sofas where we could spend the night.

'There was a good fire going, so we ordered a couple of drinks, which were brought into us as we felt the crowd at the bar was more of the "swell" type than we were. The girl who took our order looked to be a shy country girleen, about 12 years old or so.

'One of our gang, "Long Jim", was a heavy smoker. He always smoked a clay pipe; a Knockcrockery pipe, he called it, and he always carried a spare pipe in his bundle. Those pipes were made in Knockcrockery in County Roscommon and Long Jim always maintained that they were the coolest and sweetest ones in the world for a smoke.

'When the little girl saw Jim spitting on the floor while smoking, she got a spittoon and placed it on the floor in front of him. He did not know what a spittoon was so he spat to one side of it. When the girl moved the spittoon to that spot, Long Jim then began to spit to the other side. This kept going on like a game of see-saw for a while until Jim at last said, "Listen, girl, if you don't take that yoke away, I'll spit into it!"

'The girl, who had been too shy to tell him, then informed him that that was exactly what the "yoke" was designed for and we all had a good laugh.

'You know,' said Tom, 'in those days, you could buy a glass of beer for a penny farthing and a glass of good whiskey for three pence.'

Tom went on to tell me about the time he worked with a man who was a good hypnotist. His name was O'Connell and he hailed from the Mayo–Roscommon border area. One time they were 'on tramp' after finishing some harvest work in Lincoln and were on the lookout for more work.

They had been lucky enough to meet up with a farmer who had a 3-acre field of oat sheaves to be stooked and a promise of some more harvest work later. (Stooking meant putting the bound sheaves in small stooks or stacks, about twelve to sixteen sheaves in each stook.)

The harvest field was over a mile from the farmer's house and Tom Dick felt they should begin work that evening, but O'Connell told him to stop worrying and said they should head to the pub instead.

They spent the entire evening in the pub and awoke much later than intended. O'Connell told Tom not to worry and told him to stay out of sight until he had finished business with the farmer. He saw the farmer handing over the agreed price and then going off. O'Connell told him to get his bundle and to get ready for the road. After a hurried meal, they set off. The sheaves were all lying flat and it had started to rain.

O'Connell told Tom that he was a hypnotist and that he had hypnotised the farmer into believing that the field of oats was fully stooked. He added that it was lucky that the farmer was the right type as he would not have been able to do the same with everybody.

22

ALT A' CHLÉIBH

On foggy autumn mornings in Ireland, observant rural dwellers have the privilege of viewing one of the grandest sights of the otherwise hidden side of nature. The hitherto invisible spider's webs strung on hedgerows, long grass, shrubs and weeds become visible in delightful shapes and patterns owing to the settlement of fog-film over them.

On one such foggy autumn morning in the middle of the seventeenth century, two men fleeing for their lives did not view the spider's webs with gladness. They knew that the trail of broken webs left in their wake would make their pursuers' work of tracking them so much easier. The fugitives were two members of the Balla Burkes, who were known as *Burcaí an Tearmainn* or Burkes of the Termon.

In 1641 they had assisted in the taking and holding of Castlebar for the Confederates. Now, nine years later, Cromwellian troops under Sir William Coote had invaded Mayo to wreak vengeance on those who had supported the Confederates and also to engage in

special reprisals for what the state papers termed 'The Massacre off the Bridge of Shrule'.

At this bridge, a force of eighty civilian refugees and English soldiers fleeing from Castlebar were set upon by the Burkes and practically wiped out. The Protestant bishop of Castlebar, his wife and their servant alone escaped. Their lives were spared at the intercession of the local Catholic curate, Father Brian Kilkenny of Knock.

The memory of those events helped the fugitives make a greater effort as they knew the grim fate that lay in store, if captured. Coming to a shallow section of the Yellow River, they waded through it for some distance to cover their trail and then headed for the bleak village of Lackafinna on the side of Slievehorn Mountain. This village was known as *Leac a finna fine fána, gan greim ime nó braon bainne.**

In Lackafinna, they fell in with a local squatter who agreed to act as their guide. Knowing that their pursuers were not far behind, their guide led them directly to a steep gorge in the mountainside. Two freebooters of the Clan Mac Nicholas lived one on each side of the gorge. They had an ingenious system for communication and for a quick getaway if needed. A stout 'bog deal' rope was strung across the gorge and was looped at each end over a strong oaken peg, which was inclined outwards from the cliff's edge.

The rope was made of strips of bog deal, which, when twisted, made a rope capable of withstanding a high breaking strain.

A stout wickerwork basket was suspended from this rope and two lighter ropes were attached to the basket to enable it to be pulled from one side to the other if required.

If enemies approached from one end, the people in danger were hauled to the other side of the gorge and the rope was jerked off and, with the basket, hidden in the thick shrubbery until the danger had passed.

The guide lost no time in getting the Mac Nicholas brothers and their aerial ropeway into action. The two Burkes, their guide and the Mac Nicholas brother living on that side of were quickly hauled

---

* Roughly translated, this means 'Lackafinna bare and wild without a pat of butter or a dram of milk'.

across the gorge and the rope and basket were taken off and hidden before Coote's men arrived on the scene.

Peering through the fog over the cliff edge, the pursuers concluded that the fugitives had toppled over into the deep chasm and were probably lying dead at the bottom. Later, the Burke brothers doubled back on their tracks and continued their flight for some distance into Gallen, until the warm sun dispelled the fog and made the task of tracking them less easy.

From that time onwards, that remarkable canyon 3 miles northwest of Kiltimagh has been known as the Cliff of *Alt a' Chléibh*. The Mac Nicholas clan came to Mayo early in the fourteenth century and, along with another adventurer sept, the Mac Hales, acted as vassals and retainers for the powerful De Exeter Jordans. In turn, the Jordans acted as vassals to the De Burgos, or Burkes, who ruled Connacht for almost 400 years.

'The Cliff', as *Alt a' Chléibh*** was commonly called, was a favourite gathering place for the young and not so young boys and girls for two and sometimes three Sundays in late July and early August, when the bilberries or '*fraocháns*' were ripe.

The last Sunday in July was the most popular date for the purpose and was known by various names: Bilberry Sunday, Garland Sunday, *Fraochán* Sunday, Reek (Croagh Patrick) Sunday, and so on.

Another favourite spot for bilberry picking was Cloughwally*** Hill, overlooking a picturesque lake 3 miles south of the cliff. The bilberry, also known as the blueberry, is well known in the US and other countries, blueberry pie being a big favourite. A sister, acid-laden bog berry, locally called the *múnóg*, abounds in many local bogs. The same berry, known as the cranberry, is extensively propagated in the US, where cranberry sauce is popular for sauces and flavourings.

The bilberry gatherings at *Alt a' Chléibh* and Cloughwally died out over sixty years ago.

** *Alt A' Chléibh* – 'The Cliff of the Basket'

*** Cloughwally – 'Stony Village' (*Cloch Bhaile*)

23

DROICHEAD NA DTUILE

I n my early school days, I often heard old-age pensioners, on their way to Swinford to collect their pensions of two shillings a week, refer to a bridge on the road from Swinford to Tubbercurry as *Droichead na dTuile*, 'the bridge of the flood'. A man who lived 50 yards from this bridge was known as Mickey 'Bridighe' to distinguish him from others of the same surname (Groarke). Mickey was a noted fisher, fowler, poacher and storyteller.

My father had similar interests as Mickey where wildlife was concerned and they often exchanged visits and ideas to update their plans and strategies. On one occasion on which I accompanied my father, I got the history of the nearby bridge from Mickey and the reason for its watery sobriquet – *Droichead na dTuile*.

According to Mickey, the bridge, a well-built two-arched structure, was built in the 'bad times'. This probably meant the famine years. Unfortunately, 'bad times' could refer to more epochs in Irish history than 'good times'. County Grand Juries, collections of influential landlords, were responsible for county roads and bridges before County Councils and Rural District Councils came into being around the turn of the last century.

For some reason, the floor of one arch of this bridge was laid at a slightly higher level than the floor of the other arch. This meant that the higher arch would take the overflow of the other arch only when the river flooded. This arrangement resulted in this arch getting silted with sand and clay up to a height of 3 or 4 feet, so it served no useful purpose except in very high floods. In fact, the bridge up to the present day.

The local landlord did not reside in the vicinity of the bridge but on another estate some miles away. His wife was a lady who had a penchant for organising open-air parties and picnics for her friends during the summer months.

On one occasion, she accompanied her husband on a trout fishing expedition to the river in the vicinity of the 'Bridge of the Flood'. This river, the Sonnagh River, is a noted trout stream and is one of the two Moy tributaries left untouched by the recent £10 million drainage scheme. The other was the Yellow River in the Foxford area, conservation being the reason in both cases. The good lady fixed on the dry arch of the bridge as the ideal, picturesque spot for her next open-air party. She got her husband to have the soil under the bridge levelled down to a height of 2 feet above the river level and edged with flowers. Some planks or strong boards resting on boxes were installed for seating and on a fine Sunday in early summer, the party was launched in the early afternoon.

The eviction of a tenant and his weak family from his cottage about a mile upstream from the bridge a short time previously had created a great deal of local animosity for the landlord and three men with 'Ribbonmen' affiliations decided to express this local anger in a positive way. They picked a quiet, lonely spot about a half mile upstream from the bridge to construct a sod and stone dam over the river. They started operations before midnight on the night before the party, working all through the night, and by eight or nine o'clock the following morning, they had a high, strong dam across the river. Covering their footprints was no problem as they had worked in their bare feet.

They took the doors from the home of the recently evicted tenant and used them in the construction of the dam. They probably regarded this as an act of poetic justice.

The flow from two small tributaries between the dam and the bridge, coupled with the overflow over the dam, helped to give the river a normal appearance when the party started.

A sentry posted midway between the bridge and the dam, but concealed by a clump of bushes from the bridge party, gave the 'dam busters' the sign when the party was in full swing.

When the Ribbonmen got the message, they lost no time in wrecking the dam and letting the full might of the waters, which had built up over the preceding 15 to 18 hours, down on the revellers. The Ribbon Society, it is worth noting in passing, was an agrarian rights society founded to fight landlord injustice and members were so-named as they wore a small strip of ribbon inside their coat collars as a badge of recognition amongst themselves.

On the approach to the bridge, the river narrows and there is a sharp turn to the right. This, coupled with the steep sides, concealed the rushing water from the bridge party until it was almost too late.

With a wild rush to a horse-drawn carriage, they disappeared at top speed. A mopping-up party sent by the landlord the following day only saw mud and slush and some stray boards and planks. Local people who had scarcely a second spoon in their kitchens now had silver spoons, knives and forks to play with. However, they wisely kept them under cover until the storm blew over,

Once in a while, the Sonnagh River experiences flash floods in summer when thunderstorms occur higher up the river around Barnalyra Wood. With a descent of over 700 feet, these floods have often wreaked havoc. As the day of the bridge party was hot and sultry with local thundershowers, this excuse was trotted out and believed by the picnic party. By the time the real story leaked, it was too late to do much about it.

Mention of the dearth of spoons before the party brings to mind a current local joke of former days. A youth who was late for roll call was taken to task by his teacher. When asked why he was late, he gruffly replied, 'Had I a spoon, had I?' The implication in this cryptic reply was, of course, that he had to wait his turn in the queue for porridge or 'stirabout' until a spoon became available for breakfast.

Three or four miles upstream from *Droichead na dTuile* a townland along the river bears the unusual and unlikely name of Trouthill. Early in the last century, a team of Ordnance Survey engineers and

ex-British Army surveyors known as 'sappers' were busy mapping and surveying areas of the country that had previously been over-looked or unfinished.

The sapper engaged in this work along the banks of the Sonnagh River was anxious to give English names or English translations to townlands with Gaelic names.

When he came to the village of *Cnoc Breac* (Grey Hill) he asked the local landlord the English translation of the name. 'Well,' replied the landlord, 'I am not much of a Gaelic scholar, but *cnoc* means a hill and *breac* means a trout.' To this day the official name of the village or townland has been Trouthill.

24

'Fighting Fitz'

L istening in early youth to fireside tales of 'Fighting Fitz', as George Robert Fitzgerald of Turlough was locally called, I formed the opinion that he must have been a wonderful type of folk hero. As I grew older and realised that he belonged to the gambling, rack-renting, privileged landlord class implanted by Cromwell or William of Orange, his career lost much of its glamour for me.

Probably no member of the Irish Ascendancy packed in so much action, adventure, physical danger and genuine attempts to improve his estates and provide employment as Fitzgerald did in his short life of thirty-eight years. If ever a person could be called a victim of fate, Fitzgerald would be a strong contender.

At the height of his pride and popularity in 1783, he was described as the best-dressed dandy in Ireland. Yet, when he went to his execution in 1794, he was described as being dressed as a tattered peasant in a coat tied with rope and an old caubeen hat tied with a string.

Born in Turlough House, Castlebar, in the year 1748, he was the eldest son of George Fitzgerald. A second son, Lionel, did not hit the headlines – except as a spendthrift and wastrel of the average 'spoilt boy' type. George Robert's mother was formerly Lady Mary Berkely, a sister of Bishop Berkely, a noted scholar and philosopher, who was Earl of Bristol and Bishop of Derry, a post which carried an annuity of £20,000. The Fitzgerald's of Turlough were large property owners with a high rent roll. George was described as being not very tall, wiry and active, with the face of an angel but the mind of a devil.

He enjoyed jumping horses down over steep banks and quarries and into flooded rivers and waterfalls. He organised midnight fox-hunts by torchlight, which only resulted in injuries to horses and men, terrorising tenants and livestock and levelling tenants' fences.

On one occasion, he made a bet that he could walk his horse over the parapet wall of Ballylahan Bridge with the River Moy in full flood. His friend, Chris Boynes of Lakelands, Manulla, took up the bet. When Fitzgerald and his horse were halfway across the bridge, the horse took fright at a huge lump of foam in the water and plunged straight into the river.

Horse and rider were quickly swept downstream, but Fitzgerald steered him to land at the first turn in the river. 'I thought you were a goner, Fitz,' said Boynes when they met afterwards. 'Never fear,' said Fitzgerald. 'The man born to be hanged need never fear water!'

It was only later when he became part of the duelling, gambling, high-living fraternity that Fitzgerald's troubles really began. His first duel, with an army officer in Galway, was said to have affected him adversely for the rest of his life. He received a serious head wound and was unconscious for three days. Thereafter, he was troubled at times with spells of moody depression and at times with ungovernable fits of temper.

When his marriage to Lady Jane Connolly of Kildare was arranged, his father signed over a slice of the Fitzgerald property and nearby Rockfield House, plus an annuity of £6,000. Old George thought that this spelt the end of his troubles and worries on account of his spirited son.

In fact, it was only the beginning. George Robert took off to Europe on a protracted honeymoon, returning three years later. He is said to have spent £40,000, plus debts unknown, on his three-year sojourn on the Continent. He brought back a motley collection of beasts and birds, which only added to the expenses and worries on the Turlough estate. When old George refused to hand over any more money to his son, George Robert promptly locked him in a room with some of his motley pets.

The enforced company of the foul-smelling, verminous bear was believed to have broken down the resolve of his father, as George Robert is said to have got promises or promissory notes that solved his immediate problems. He ordered his wines direct from France and the wine carts travelling from Turlough to Westport Quay to transport them were a common sight.

In one of his constructive moods, when he felt there was a future for flax growing and linen production in the area, he took tradesmen-weavers, spinners, hacklers, etc., from Northern Ireland and built houses for them in Turlough. He encouraged flax growing in a big way. Unfortunately, his plans were not as successful as he had hoped. His unstable nature and his having too many irons in the fire, together with too many incompetent advisers, proved to be big drawbacks.

At the great Volunteer Convention in Dungannon in 1783, George Robert may be said to have reached the zenith of his power and popularity. He was in command of the Review Force of the huge Volunteer muster there. His uncle was one of the two leading candidates for the post of Supreme Commander of the Volunteers, the other being the Earl of Charlemont. Fitzgerald's uncle, the bishop, was described as arriving at the convention in a coach and six with silver-mounted harness and purple ribbons flying.

Charlemont won the scramble for 'pelf and power', to quote one account, and needless to say it meant little difference to the hewers of wood and the drawers of water. Had his uncle won, George Robert probably would have been given a lucrative post, which might have changed the whole course of his career. Instead, his return to Mayo and his mounting debts spelt disaster. His frequent duels, however, went merrily on. He fought two duels, which were regarded as inconclusive, with 'Humanity' Dick Martin of Connemara and Caesar French of Oughterard.

In all, he is believed to have fought between fifty and sixty duels. Local legend gives the figure as 100, which is most likely an exaggeration. He fought his third duel in Paris while on his honeymoon, receiving a leg wound, which led to him limping ever after.

On one occasion, Fitz borrowed 100 guineas from the Kiltimagh landlord, 'Minor' Browne of Newtownbrowne.

Seeing no hope of repayment, Browne paid a personal call on Fitzgerald.

Guessing the reason for the call, Fitzgerald took him out to the shooting gallery after dinner. Fitzgerald had an auger-hole an inch in diameter drilled through a tree in the midst of some shrubbery. Measuring twenty paces, he took careful aim and fired his bullet through the auger-hole.

Browne, like many young landlords' sons, had spent a term in the British army and was the crack shot of his regiment. He asked Fitzgerald for a nail, which he drove partway into the tree. He then took aim and hit the nail squarely on the head.

Fitzgerald decided that a duel would not solve his problems, so he sent Browne home with a hunting colt in lieu of the debt. The general belief locally was that Fitzgerald never fired through the auger-hole but into the shrubbery beside the tree.

Early in 1786, and with mounting debts, Fitzgerald was most anxious to secure the lucrative post of the command of the Mayo Volunteers. These were, of course, the Volunteers under Grattan's Parliament, where money was spent lavishly.

His main opponent for the post was a neighbour, Patrick Randal McDonnell of Chancery Hall, which, to annoy Fitzgerald, he renamed 'Liberty Hall'. Fitzgerald had his Turlough Volunteers, locally dubbed the Turlough Militia, which were more of a liability than an asset.

The County Sheriff, Denis Browne, was a sworn enemy of Fitzgerald's, so it came as no surprise that McDonnell got the post. Fitzgerald had once challenged Browne to a duel and had taken a pot shot at him at Westport Quay. As Fitzgerald's name was next on the list for the appointment, he, in his misguided rage, saw the elimination of McDonnell as the solution to his problem.

One of his shady advisers was a discredited lawyer, a Welshman named Timothy Brecknock. Fitzgerald was a magistrate and as such had the powers of arrest. Brecknock's advice to him was to arrest McDonnell on some trumped-up charge, arrange a rescue attempt, and then shoot him.

Under English law a magistrate had the authority to order the shooting of a legally held prisoner to prevent a rescue from custody. Another character in the plot was a general manager for Fitzgerald, Andy Craig, known as 'Scotch' Andy. Sir Henry Lynch-Blosse of Balla had previously employed him.

However, the plans were discussed too freely and somebody at the last moment informed McDonnell. McDonnell is believed to have tried to get to the military base in Swinford, as the road into Castlebar was too well watched by the Turlough Militia. He was arrested in Ballyvary and in the fake rescue attempt in Turlough was shot dead by Scotch Andy.

When the news spread, the military in Castlebar decided to steal a march on Fitzgerald, as they expected a hot reception in arresting him otherwise. They slipped into the house noiselessly and found Fitzgerald unarmed, but he grabbed a heavy silver candlestick and then backed into a narrow porch where only one assailant at a time could follow.

He defended himself by parrying the sword thrusts with the heavy candlestick until his arm became too swollen and painful. It is believed that the orders of Browne were to take him alive.

The names of the twelve members of the jury make for interesting reading. In Faulkner's *Life of Fitzgerald*, they are given as follows: John Moore, Ballintaffy; William Lindsay, Hollymount; Thomas Ormsby,

Ballinamore; James Lynch, Clogher; Smith Steele, Foxford; John Joyce, Oxford; William Ousley, Rushbrook; Joseph Lambert, Togher; Christopher Boynes, Lakelands; James Miller, Westport; James Gildea, Crosslough, and William Ellison, Tallyho Lodge.

In addition to Fitzgerald, Brecknock, Craig and a minor accessory named Fulton were charged with murder. Craig turned King's evidence, which was the official term for turning informer, and his life was spared. Before Craig fired the fatal shot, McDonnell, according to local tradition, offered him 100 of his greenest acres to spare his life. A verdict of guilty was returned against Fitzgerald, Brecknock and Fulton and all were sentenced to be hanged.

The day of Fitzgerald's execution was a day of intermittent spells of rain, thunder and lightning so violent that many superstitious people stayed indoors. Executions in those days took place on the corner of the Mall, opposite the main gateway to the military barracks.

When all was ready for George Robert's execution, after spending some time in prayer, he leaped impetuously from the scaffold, breaking both the rope and a leg. According to local tradition, he shouted, 'My life is my own!'

'Not while there is a rope in Castlebar,' was the grim retort of Denis Browne.

When his body was taken to Turlough House to be waked, there were no silver candlesticks left, so candles had to be stuck in bottles. In the spell between his arrest and trial, mobs had invaded Turlough House and taken everything of value. With Fitzgerald having fallen foul of the authorities, little was done to prevent this wholesale vandalism. George Robert's family consisted of one daughter. Her mother, the former Lady Jane Connolly, died a few years before her husband. All their family lives were said to be happy as could be.

Their daughter was raised with her mother's people, the Conollys of Castletown House, County Kildare, but died while still a young girl. Some believe that she accidentally came across an account of her father's life and death in the library there and it so affected her that it hastened her untimely death.

Local tradition asserted that a few minutes before George Robert Fitzgerald's execution a horseman was seen approaching Castlebar on the Dublin road, trying to urge on his tired horse and waving a piece of paper in his hand. Denis Browne, according to the story, speeded up the execution. The paper in question was believed to be a pardon for Fitzgerald from the Lord Lieutenant, but nothing further was heard of the matter.

Spencer Street and Station Road were not built-up areas at the time, so a horseman approaching the Mall on the Dublin road could be observed as they travelled the last few hundred yards east of the Mall.

25

SEEING GHOSTS?

Some time ago, I was questioned by a grandson as to whether I had ever seen a ghost. My reply was in the negative. 'However,' I continued, 'I felt close to seeing one on a couple of occasions.' That answer did not let me off the hook, so to be more specific I related the following two or three anecdotes to him, all of which happened to be true.

'When,' I commenced, 'I was in my middle teens I was returning alone from a small country house dance sometime after midnight. Not far from a lonely landmark known for generations as the "Black Gate", I came to a crossroads, or rather a branch road, that had a reputation for generations of being haunted, even on some occasions in broad daylight. As I approached this spot, I began to dwell on some of the eerie tales I had heard about it.

'A man was said to have been killed by a neighbour beside the road at this junction. This happened during one of the lesser potato famines preceding the Great Famine of 1847. In those days, and in some parts of Ireland down to our time, land was held from the landlords in a kind of communal occupation called the Rundale system. The landlords did not favour high, earthen fences, which they regarded as a waste of land.

'As the tenants were ticket-of-leave people who could be evicted at a day's notice, they had to agree to this arrangement. The line of demarcation therefore was a small token fence about a foot wide and a foot and a half high, called in Gaelic a *cealóid*.

'With a teeming rural population and at a time when our peerless Goldsmith reckoned 'that every rood maintained its man', there were no waste headlands. Every inch right up to the *cealóid* was tilled. On one occasion a man came early to dig out his potato allotment at the spot I have mentioned during a lean famine period. He found his next-door neighbour tunnelling under the *cealóid*, or dividing fence, to take his potatoes from his allotment. A fight with the two 'loys', or heavy, cumbersome spades, ensued, resulting in one man's death and the transporta-tion of the other man to Van Diemen's Land – a penal colony now known as Tasmania.

'Local people for a long time afterwards avoided that place after nightfall, some asserting that they had seen the dead man and his loy there. About 100 years later, a cousin of my mother's, who was a card-playing fanatic, was returning home in the small hours of the morning from one of his many late-night, and sometimes all-night, card games.

'When he came to this reputedly haunted spot, the moon was shining brightly so he never dreamed he would see anything ghostly or eerie.

'To his surprise, his dog seemed to enter into a savage fight with an unseen adversary. The dog snapped and snarled, even standing on his hind legs at times and swaying from side to side. He finally broke into a run for home about a quarter of a mile away. When his owner came along and opened the door, he dashed in and got under the bed, where he stayed trembling until daylight. His owner gave up his late-night card games from that night onwards.

'As my mind travelled back to those days, I felt a little puz-zled, to say the least, to see two bright, glowing spots on the grass margin of the road, spaced at the right distance to resemble two eyes. I stamped my foot on the road in case it might be a cat or some other small nocturnal animal. With a certain amount of cau-tion and uneasiness, I crept closer and grabbed one of the "eyes". I found a sticky substance in my hand that stopped glowing.

'As the night was very dark, I postponed further examination and wrapped the substance in a handkerchief, examining it by daylight the next day. I found it to be old, decayed timber, which gives a phosphorescent glow when placed in a very dark place at night.

'An old tree said to be a rare type of poplar was blown down at this road junction some years previously. Being useless for firewood and being no obstruction lying on a broad grass margin, it was left to decay there.

'Was that the only time you nearly saw a ghost?' asked my youthful question master.

'Well,' I continued, 'about forty years ago, I can remember a warm day I spent helping an uncle of mine harvesting oats. He lived about 10 miles away. He worked late into the night to finish the programme. When leaving for home, my aunt sent two large buckets of apples with me. I secured the apples in a light canvas bag on the carrier of my bike.

'The night was warm and heavy and I ran into several thunderstorms, from which I had to shelter in dwelling houses and other buildings on the way home.

'When I got to the railway bridge outside Swinford, it was past midnight. I found the roadway under the bridge flooded to a depth of 2 or maybe 3 feet. This left me no choice but to detour by the roadway that went by the ancient churchyard of Kilconduff.

'Seven hundred years previously, "marauding foreigners" (according to local tradition) murdered the resident priest there. His faithful black hound stood by his body for two or three days and when the marauders returned by the same route the hound fiercely attacked them. They eventually killed it.

'The spot was named from that time onwards as *Cille Chon Dubh* – the grave, or churchyard, of the black hound. Kilconduff is frequently mentioned in the old annals as a turbulent spot in the wars between the natives and the "foreigners", dating back to the thirteenth century. Needless to say, it carried the reputation down through the years of being haunted.

'I was remembering those details as I was cycling past the churchyard gate when I thought I heard a light footstep right beside me and, at intervals, two more footsteps.

'I braked and jumped off the bike. As the night was dark, I took the battery-operated lamp and shone it on the ground around me

along the road. I saw a large apple on the road and retracing my tracks I found two more. When I examined the bag of apples on the bike I found a hole, probably caused by the bumpy, sandy, pot-holed road and the sharp carrier. So that explained the "footsteps"!

'Two or three years after this event, I was cycling to a road construction job on the Irishtown–Dalgan road, 20 miles distant from my home. It was a fine spring morning at about 6 a.m. As I came to the Ballinamore Wood near Linbawn Bridge (now cut away), visibility was good, up to maybe 200 yards. At a gap in the roadside fence about 20 or 30 yards in front of me, a stoat crossed the road and entered by a gap on the opposite side into the wood. He was carrying a dead stoat in his mouth. He was followed by a dozen or more stoats travelling slowly in an orderly single file. I felt, and to this day feel convinced, that I had the privilege of witnessing a stoat's funeral. Like his English and Scottish cousin, the weasel, the stoat is regarded among rural dwellers with a good deal of superstition, because so little is known of his lifestyle.'

There was a belief that a stoat's spit was very poisonous and that if it came into contact with a raw cut, death would ensue within three days.

On one occasion, when I was 10 or 11 years old and walking on long grass by a fence, I came to a halt on hearing screams at my feet.

On looking down, I saw that I had stood on a young stoat, which was screaming and spitting. I jumped aside quickly and was glad to see him disappear through the long grass.

I was wearing knee-length trousers, the usual schoolboy's wear at the time. Even so, despite my youthful bravado, I was nevertheless happy when the next three days passed and I was still alive.

26

KILCONDUFF IN LOCAL TRADITION

While the official name of Swinford parish is Kilconduff, there exists no corresponding townland of the same name hereabouts for reference in tracing the origins of such a unique name for a parish. Neighbouring parishes such as Killedan, Kilcolman, Kilmovee, Toomore, etc., differ from Kilconduff in this regard.

The churchyard of Kilconduff, from which the parish derives its name, is located at the centre and highest point of Rathscanlon townland. Naming parishes to commemorate some saint of the Celtic Church has been the most popular form of parish nomenclature in Ireland.

Finding saints' names for the purpose should not have been too difficult when we consider that, for instance, over forty saints of the old Celtic Church bore the name of Colman. According to local belief in the Aran Islands, over 120 saints of the old Celtic Church are interred in the little churchyard of Killeany.

Most of those old saints (many of them believed to have been among the foremost scholars of their day) are said to have come there to end their days in private seclusion and contemplation. How those dedicated people managed to survive in such harsh, inhospitable surroundings puzzles the imagination. They could not even depend on locusts and wild honey, which were the mainstay for the Israelite anchorites of old. Needless to say, unlike the Israelites of old, they had no Golden Calf to worship should they feel so inclined.

Incidentally, the Golden Calf of Israelite tradition would be worth a 'dig', to use a materialistic American phrase, if its whereabouts could be guessed. Leaving the location and the value of the Golden Calf to tradition and the computer, we will return to the slightly more straightforward realms of local tradition.

Early in the twelfth century, according to local tradition, the friar in residence at his little church on the site of the present Kilconduff churchyard was slain by a marauding band.

In addition to the constant warfare between Norman colonists and the native Irish for over 400 years, there were non-aligned armed bands, to use a modern expression, whose main objective was plunder. Monasteries and churches suffered in a big way before the Reformation and legitimised such acts.

The robbers who killed the friar returned using the same route some days later and were fiercely attacked by the friar's black wolfhound. After a fierce struggle, they succeeded in killing the hound and buried him beside the friar. From that time onwards, the place was called *Cille Chon Dubh* – the Church of the Black Hound.

From the early twelfth century onwards, Kilconduff is frequently mentioned in the old annals in connection with the ever-recurring warfare between the Norman and Welsh adventurers on the one hand and the native Celts on the other. The division was not always so clear-cut in those turbulent days, as on occasions some natives sided with the foreigners and at other times Normans who had intermarried with natives sided with them against fresh Normans sent over from England to supersede them.

The murder of the Kilconduff friar is not mentioned in the old annals but the killing of Meachair O Ruadháin is. He was killed at the door of his church in Kilsheshnan, by the foreigners, only 3 or 4 miles from Kilconduff. The O Ruadháin clan (Ruanes) was a ruling class in Kilsheshnan (Killasser) at the time.

In addition to O Ruadháin, other named local clans in the old annals include O'Hara, O'Higgins, O'Hennigan, O'Moráin and Mac Duarcain (Durkin). While not as numerous as of yore, perhaps, all these surnames are still to be found locally up to the present time.

A famous prophesy made wishfully by the *London Times* over 100 years ago has yet to be fulfilled. This was the forecast that 'the Celtic Irishman will soon be as rare in Connemara as the Red Indian on the Plains of Manhattan'.

27

KILLASSER MYSTERIES

Over 200 years ago, in 1778, the English traveller, writer and farming expert, Arthur Young, toured Ireland. He made a brief reference to the East Mayo parish of Killasser.

'In this parish,' he wrote, 'I have found some of the best land in Mayo bordered by some of the worst land in the world.'

Killasser's St Lasser's church is so-named after a saint of the early Irish Church founded by St Patrick. Between Ballyfarnon and Carrick-on-Shannon, on a sloping elevation, adjacent to one of the most beautiful of Irish lakes, Lough Key, there is a blessed well dedicated to St Lasser.

It is a place of pilgrimage around the 15 August, a popular time for local pilgrimages in Ireland. Nearby are Kilronan churchyard and abbey, where O'Carolan, the last of the old Irish bards, lies buried.

The road leads from the main Swinford–Foxford road near Cloongullane Bridge (on the Moy) to Croghan Hill, the highest point of the parish of Killasser.

The Norman invaders and their allies, referred to in the old Irish annals as 'the foreigners', were adept at discovering prime land. They figure in the history of Killasser as early as 1236.

In his book *A Topographical Dictionary of Ireland*, published over 180 years ago, Samuel Lewis mentioned a bloody war fought in Killasser in earlier times between the native O'Rowans and the

Norman Jordans. This battle, according to Lewis, was so bloody that the battleground was known as Lugnafulla – the hollow of blood.

O'Rowan is a variation in translation of O'Ruadhain, the ruling clan in Killasser in days of old. The location of Lugnafulla remains a mystery today. A townland, whose official name is Dromada, seems to be the most likely guess.

This townland is still called locally by its older name of Lug na h-Achaidh, pronounced Lognahauha (sometimes shortened to Lognahaw), which means the hollow of the fortified field.

The *Annals of Lough Key* record that Meachair O Ruadháin was slain by the 'foreigners' at the door of his church in Kilshesnan. Kilsheshnan (*Cill Saicsnean*) has been bracketed with Killasser but that location is also not known today. The date given in the annals is AD 1263.

The peak of that hill still retains its old name of Srón Cam. The date recorded for that battle is AD 1328. The exact location is no longer known today.

Near the border separating the parishes of Killasser and Attymass/Coolcarney and close to the Eagle's Rock lies the picturesque old-world village of Glendaduff. '*Gleann dhá Ghuth*' – the glen of the two voices (echoes) – is sometimes incorrectly spelt 'Glenduff'.

The old annals record O'Donnell of Tirconnell and his Ulstermen invaded Connacht on a cattle-raiding foray and, at a battle at Cruachan Gailing, slew the local chieftain, O Ruadháin, before retreating northwards again. Cruachan Gailing is Croghan Mountain in Killasser.

In one of their frequent raids into Carra, which was for-eigner's territory, the Mc.Donoghs of Ballymote and their allies, the Mc.Dermotts, were pursued by Mac William Burke and his Gallowglasses.

In an action at Glendaduff, the raiders repulsed their pursuers. To avoid a confrontation with the O'Haras of Belclare, who were preparing to protect their cattle stocks, the McDonogh/McDermott force seized a local herdsman to guide them over the mountain to Attymass. Being lame, he could not get away in time like his neigh-bours. He was called *Cathal Bacach* (Lame Cahal).

This route over the mountain, over which Lame Cahal guided the cattle raiders, is known to this day as '*Staighre Cathail Bhacaigh*' (Lame Cahal's mountain path or stairway).

This path, visible for a distance of 20 miles, is getting fainter every year due to the decrease in pedestrian traffic over the mountain. It is easier nowadays to sit in a car and go round the road.

28

FUN OF THE FAIR

Like most long-established fairs, the fair in Swinford on the first Wednesday of every month was more than just a market for the buying, selling and exchange of livestock. It was a Mecca for tradesmen and handymen who came from a wide area to sell their wares.

Fish, fresh and salted, cockles, dilisk and other produce of the sea were there in abundance, chiefly in spring and early summer.

Fair evenings were regarded as a social event by the young and the not so young. Ballad singers and musicians, acrobats and gamblers, confidence tricksters and medicine quacks helped to contribute to all the fun of the fair. Fairs were lucky places for the arrangement of rural marriages and in some places semi-professional matchmakers did their part.

Like most Irish garrison towns, Swinford had its ghetto-like district, known as 'The Lane'. Here, ex-soldiers and ex-militiamen thrown on the scrapheap of human misery by their imperial masters existed rather than lived. Fishing, doing odd jobs and catching goldfinches and other songbirds with some bird lime in decoy cages were the main sources of income to supplement their meagre pensions of 4 pennies a day.

There were cheap rooms and lodging houses in 'The Lane' where long-distance chancers sometimes stayed on the night before Swinford fair. Many of them got away to an early start after the fair as some of their items and wares would not stand up to much investigation.

I can remember, as a youngster, hearing an inhabitant of the Lane known as Old Neddy tell of his experience with two shady lodgers around the turn of the last century.

'One night before the fair,' said Old Neddy, 'two brothers called for lodgings. After I agreed, they asked leave to use the kitchen fire and a large boiling saucepan for an hour or two. They carried two large battered-looking suitcases.

'One of them took several dozen empty ointment boxes out of one case and the other brother took several bars of Sunlight soap out of the other.

'Some of the boxes were very small and would hold little more than a spoonful of ointment or a similar substance, while the larger ones were three or four times bigger. After boiling the soap they filled it into the boxes after adding some light powder to kill the soapy smell, as one of the brothers told me. Next morning, they took all the boxes to the fair and set up their stalls on either side of the street. I gave each of them a herring box and a square of old tarpaulin to do for stalls.

'One of them took the larger boxes to his stall and left the smaller ones to his brother. I had no interest in the fair so I went off to the Moy fishing as a salmon or even a perch for dinner would suit me better than loafing around corners.

'I returned as the boyos were coming in from the fair and were getting a mug of tea before moving on to Charlestown for the fair the following day. I asked them how they got on at the fair and they said that they had done very well and had sold all their stuff. I casually asked them the reason for packing some of this stuff in small boxes and some of it in the larger ones. I said I supposed that they had two different prices.

'The man who had the larger boxes said that he had sold his stuff as a remover of stains from clothes. "You know," he said, "blue serge is getting very popular and is easily stained. Anyone I saw in the crowd wearing serge I called him up and damped any spot I saw with a wet cloth, maybe some spots that had no stains at all. I then rubbed in a little of the 'stain remover' and told him not to brush it off for 12 hours. I felt that was giving me plenty of time to get out of town!"

'The other brother then chimed in and said that he had less trouble selling his stuff. He just told them that it was the latest remedy for corns and bunions. Half the people at the fair must have had corns or bunions, the way they limped.'

Old Neddy said that he did not meet the two brothers again until a year later.

He walked to Croaghpatrick for the annual pilgrimage on the last Sunday of July. This day was variously known as Reek Sunday, Garland Sunday or *Fraochán* Sunday.

Beside the St Patrick statue at the base of the mountain, he saw the two brothers selling medals of St Patrick as fast as they could hand them out, while solemnly swearing that they had been blessed by His Holiness, the Pope.

Two regular patrons of Swinford Fair in those days were former members of a circus. When they reached middle age and their strength and their eyesight began to slip, they were let go. They were no longer able for the exacting circus life. At the fair they gave exhibitions of strength, skill and human endurance, such as treading barefoot or lying bareback on boards studded with nails 3 inches long, or allowing flagstones to be broken with sledgehammers on their bare chests as they lay on the wet, guttery streets.

I can faintly remember seeing them walking around the streets with their heads thrown back: one had a heavy, iron-shod wheel from a cart balanced on the bridge of his nose; his comrade balanced a similar object on his chin. That those unfortunate men earned their donations over and over again goes without saying.

THE RIBBONMEN

T he Ribbonman captain, Roger Keane, more popularly
known as 'Rory of the Hill', is still remembered in his
native West Mayo parish of Kilgeever even though over
140 years have passed since, in his own words, he made it hot for
'landlords, middlemen and grabbers'.

At the same time that Roger was doing his part for agrarian
reform and redress, another Ribbonman leader, Seán Prendergast,
nicknamed Seán *na mBaintreach* (the widow's Seán), was operating
along similar lines in South Mayo.

Seán was known locally as the man who 'lepped the Shannon',
which was a sizeable exaggeration. Being called to assist in a puni-
tive expedition against an obnoxious Roscommon landlord, Seán
found himself surrounded by enemies while rounding up some
of the landlord's cattle. He was mounted on a very good hunting
mare of his own. Seeing himself cornered, Seán had no alternative
but to force his mare to make a seemingly impossible jump over
a good-sized tributary of the Shannon. Amazingly, Seán's mount
cleared the river and took him to safety.

On another occasion, he was surprised in one of his favourite hiding places, the ruined castle of Ballyhowley between
Claremorris and Knock. Whenever he stayed there, he placed a
carpet of hay or long grass on the ground directly under the top-
storey window in the west gable of the castle. This was to facilitate
a quick getaway if the need arose. On this occasion, hearing his

enemies rushing up the stairs, Seán coolly leapt down onto his landing pad and into the nearby Rockfield River, which was in full flood.

Being a good swimmer, he dived and allowed himself to be carried for some distance downstream before surfacing. He got away to safety while his enemies were still searching the castle.

Seán was a relative of Francis French of Rockfield Cottage, Claremorris, who was executed in Castlebar in 1799 for possessing an incriminating letter referring to the United Irish Rising of 1798. He was executed on the same day as Father Conroy. He was an ancestor of the Mossbrook Frenches.

Once, Roger spent the night in a deserted fisherman's hut on Tollaghbawn strand. The little shack was completely devoid of furniture of any sort except for a rough-and-ready bedstead and a tub of fisherman's grease that doubled as a seat.

As Roger stood waiting for daylight, looking out through cracks in the timber walls, he spied a number of figures stealthily approaching his sleeping place. From the way they were running from one sand dune to another and crouching down, he realised that they were locals who knew the area and who didn't want him to become aware of their presence.

Straight away, he knew they were scouts for a detachment of soldiers sent to arrest him. Even as he stood and watched, he could see other shadowy shapes in the half-light moving into position and encircling the hut.

The situation looked dire. As he looked desperately around him for some means of escape, the tub of grease caught his eye. An idea struck him. Hastily divesting himself of his clothes, he liberally smeared grease over all of his body and stood crouching just inside the door.

He waited until his would-be captors were just about to charge and then he threw open the door and quickly jumped aside. As he hoped, his enemies were taken completely unawares and were thrown into utter confusion. Those who were close enough to see the door opening fired their guns, which only served to add to the confusion, as the main body of soldiers had not yet got into position and had no idea of what was going on in the still murky light.

Several foes grabbed but failed to hold their intended prisoner, who slipped through their hands and away. They found that they could not manipulate their guns as speedily as they would like owing to the grease on their hands. By the time they fired a ragged volley, their quarry was out of reach.

Even though Roger ran for 3 miles to reach the house of a bachelor uncle near Killadoon on a bitter frosty night, he contracted no cold or flu. Evidently the heavy coating of grease provided him with insulation against cold and frostbite.

Many years ago, I heard an old man from the Creggauns singing a song commemorating the exploits of 'Rory of the Hill' (Roger). I can only remember the lines,

> We'll rout them all from Thallabawn
> Said Rory of the Hill.

The man from the Creggauns told me that he heard that the cream of the stick-fighting fraternity always wore leathern thongs on their wrists, which were attached to their duelling sticks at the 'grip' point. This was to ensure that they did not drop their sticks when, as often happened, a blow on the knuckles or elbow numbed their leading arm.

In addition to being a crack shot with the uncertain type of small firearms circulating in those days, Roger Keane was a redoubtable antagonist in a stick fight. Stick fighting was a pastime that lingered on in the Murrisk barony long after it was forgotten in the rest of the county.

Oddly enough, Murrisk, under the repressive Brownes of Westport and their vassals, was the first barony in Mayo to lose the Irish language.

An old man from Kilgeever gave me a rough example of the stick-fighting techniques handed down to him by his grandfather. The weapon, usually a stick about 3½ feet long, was grasped by the operator slightly nearer to one end than the other. The long end of the stick was used as a weapon of offence and the short end to parry the blows or thrusts of the assailant. Considerable skill and dexterity were called for. Sometimes when the game got out of hand, deadly wild swinging replaced the thrust and parry with sometimes fatal results.

30

WHEN RED HUGH CAME TO TAWIN ISLAND

I t had been stated that no one figure in Irish history packed so much action into his short, warlike career as 'Red' Hugh O'Donnell. The real driving force behind him was his mother, Inghín Dubh. Being the daughter of the Scottish chief Aengus Mac Donnell, of the Isles, she could call on hosts of Scottish 'Redshanks', which she regularly did. In this regard she was probably a greater thorn in England's side than the inconsistent, uncertain Granuaile.

Like most warlords of old, winter seems to have been Red Hugh's open season for his numerous campaigns. Even the epic march of O'Neill and O'Donnell to Kinsale was accomplished during a record spell of frost, which enabled them to march over hitherto impassable swamps and shallow lakes. It seems probable that the main reason for this lay in the fact that beef was the staple food for armies in the field or on the move in former times.

There were no fridges or deep-freeze containers of old, so summer campaigns meant huge losses in food, especially meat. Huge cattle raids and accompanying herds of cattle were a feature of warring armies in former times.

In Red Hugh's deepest incursion into Connacht in 1597, he took Athenry and demolished its walls. He encircled Galway but lifted the siege for lack of siege guns and scaling ladders. While besieging Galway, he was informed that the inhabitants of Tawin Island and the adjoining mainland had lost all their cattle in an epidemic of *galar pheist rubaill* (tail worm disease). Cattle suffering from any painful internal ailment will show their displeasure by continuously swishing their tail. People down through the ages have mistakenly believed that a worm in the tail was responsible for the trouble.

I have seen an old man, many years ago, make an incision in a heifer's tail and insert garlic and unsalted butter as a remedy for the *peist rubaill* disease. (*Peist rubaill* was a derisory term of old for a small, truculent person.) Red Hugh replaced the cattle with ones from his own herds of seized planters' cattle and ones taken from lukewarm Gaelic clans, chiefly the O'Haras of Belclare, the Conroys of Mayo and septs of the De Burgos and O'Malleys.

Before his return back to Ulster from Kilmaine, he spent Christmas 1595 in Brize Castle, within a few yards of the modern 'Beaten Path' entertainment complex.

Brize, referred to in the old annals as 'the strong town and castle of the Brees', was captured by the McDonoughs of Ballymote and the McDermotts in earlier times from the McMorris-Prendergasts and burned.

Brize had a feudally established cattle fair for centuries until the Lynch-Blosses superseded it with the fair of Balla, which became the second most important fair in Connacht after Ballinasloe. There was a tradition that Red Hugh and some of his men spent part of their time in Brize in field sports on the castle *bán*.

One sport, in which Red Hugh excelled, was a game akin to modern leapfrog. In this game, requiring two competitors, one man stood in a half-stooping position. His comrade, after retreating 30 or 40 yards, ran at top speed and leapt over the stooping man, resting his hands on the other's back to propel himself ahead when passing over him.

The route of Red Hugh back home is pointed out over the hill of Crucksbullagadawn and onto Ballylahan castle and from thence to Ardnaree. He is believed to have returned to the north after this campaign with over 4,000 head of seized cattle.

In 1593, two years earlier, he had advanced south as far as Kilmaine in South Mayo. On a commanding hill there he had all the leading Connacht clans assemble and pledge support for his campaign against the 'Heretic Queen'.

In 1598 Red Hugh fought alongside Hugh O'Neill at the Battle of the Yellow Ford. His army on that occasion included 1,000 Connacht men, drawn largely from the numerous De Burgo septs.

A game of leapfrog in the grounds of Ballintubber Abbey ended all interest in life for Tibóid-na-Loing, the 'sleeveen' son of Granuaile who was later made Viscount Mayo in 1627 for 'devoted service to the Crown'. In 1629 he decided to visit Ballintubber Abbey to attend the annual pattern day there. This day was partly a day of remembrance for the dead, culminating with field sports and music. When the leapfrogging began, Tiobóid-na-Loing decided to take part. Being no longer young, he called on a young, hunchbacked man, known locally as Diarmeen Cruchtach (little crooked Dermot) to be his partner. Diarmeen belonged to a sept of the De Burgos who had suffered death and deprivation at the hands of Tiobóid in earlier times when he had sided with Queen Elizabeth.

Diarmeen felt that Tiobóid wanted to make a laughing stock of him and his disability. As Tiobóid was sailing over his back, Diarmeen felled him with an upward thrust of a short dagger that he had concealed in his sleeve, a thrust that proved fatal. For centuries after, *Turas Thibóid-na-Luing leat go Baile an Tobair* (May you have the journey of Theobald of the Ships to Ballintubber) was a feared and much used curse in Mayo.

For Red Hugh's visit to Tawin Island, I am indebted to the late Freda Evans of Fairhill Road, Galway, RIP. I got the account of Tibóid-na-Loing's death from Fr Michael P. O'Flanagan, RIP, when he visited Chicago in 1932. He was a former vice president of the Sinn Féin organisation and was engaged in an unofficial capacity in Dublin researching John O'Donovan's papers when he came across this anecdote.

31

THE SOUPER'S
LITTLE COW

From social, economic and spiritual viewpoints, one of the most controversial figures in the West of Ireland from 1831 to 1883 was the Reverend Edward Nangle.

Born near Athboy, County Meath, he took up a religious career after leaving Trinity College, Dublin. A tireless worker, he was all-Ireland representative for a Dublin firm of printers supplying a seemingly endless supply of religious tracts and pamphlets. In addition to this, he acted as secretary to the Protestant School Society of Ireland. These posts, coupled with his duties as an evangelical clergyman, proved too much and he had a temporary breakdown in health. On his recovery, he travelled west and rented the island of Achill from the landlord, Sir Richard O'Donnel.

He founded in Achill a church, a school, a hospital and a printing and publishing business. He published a huge amount of propagandist tracts and pamphlets attacking 'The Idolatry of Rome'.

He also published a newspaper, the *Achill Missionary Herald and Western Witness*. His writings and sermons had a forceful, abrasive style for which he incurred (and enjoyed) the hostility of both Catholic and Protestant clergy. During the worst years of the famine (1845–8), he was often attacked for diverting monies intended for relief to his missionary activities, which included his 'souper' policy.

This meant giving free soup to the starving peasants to encourage religious conversions. On one occasion, one of his boilers for preparing soup was hidden by 'idolators'. Undaunted, the Revd Nangle had small portions of raw beef doled out to his 'customers' while awaiting another boiler from Galway.

Some days later, one of his agents came across a bunch of juveniles playing a type of football game. Many of the players were barefooted and wearing the kilt-like smock, which was standard wear for many juveniles in rural areas in those days. The agent thought that they were kicking around a young hedgehog, or *gráinneóg*. When he inquired about this, one youngster said, 'We are kicking the devil out of the Protestant beef.' A tough-looking lump of gristle and sinews bore out his statement. The agent reckoned that their mothers were to blame.

'They cooked their share of the little cow too fast,' he said. 'Tell them to cook it slower the next time.'

From that time on, local people, when they were presented with very tough meat or some other similarly tough substance, referred to it as being 'as tough as Nangle's little cow'.

I remember a travelling butcher using the phrase in the 1940s when selling beef to a housewife, who asked him if the beef was good. He laughingly replied, 'Well, as Nangle's man said, the little cow is alright.' Despite the souper slant to his activities, Nangle persevered and gave a good deal of temporary relief and doubtless saved many lives. By 1853 he was reckoned to have almost one third of the teeming population of the island converted. His success was a constant source of worry to John McHale, the Roman Catholic Archbishop of Tuam. McHale visited the island in 1853 and

established a Franciscan Third Order community in Bunnacurry, in addition to bringing more priests to the island.

A local pious lady met an easy-going character named Manus na Gug[*] one day around that time. She said that Nangle's race would be cut short soon as God was sending more priests to the island. 'I think,' responded Manus, 'that if God sent a good crop of potatoes instead, that would be the best way to stop Nangle.'

As if in answer to his prayer, there was a good crop of potatoes that year and a repeat the following year with the result that Nangle's converts reduced to a third of the number. Nangle later left on promotion to the rectorship of Skreen in North Sligo.

He astounded his friends and critics by buying out the Achill Island estate from his former landlord, Sir Richard O'Donnel, in the Encumbered Estates' Court. The price of £17,500 was regarded as a colossal sum in those days. (This purchase eventually led to him spending the last years of his life in violent opposition to Michael Davitt's Land League.) Among his other accomplishments, he was also a fluent Irish speaker and he published a decent work entitled *An Introduction to the Irish Language*.

When a new courthouse was being built on Achill Sound in 1939, I saw a 40-gallon pot-like boiler being used for boiling tar or asphalt for roof work. I was informed that it was one of Parson Nangle's soup boilers and that it was over 90 years old. I wonder where that interesting 'relic of oul' dacency' is today.

---

[*] The word 'gug' was a sort of Gaelic slang for an egg. The word was associated with Manus owing to his ability to locate wild birds' nests and drink the eggs, which, no doubt, helped to supplement the ration of thin soup.

32

SHAUN NA SOGGARTH

I rish history over the last 300 years has produced no character more universally hated and execrated in the west of Ireland than the man known as *Seán na Sagart* (often phonetically spelt as Shaun na Soggarth). His real name was John Mullowney (in modern times this would be Maloney).

Despite his infamous notoriety, comparatively little is known of his early life. This may be due in part to the fact that children were forbidden to mention his name and grown up people blessed themselves or muttered an imprecation, or maybe both. When young aspirants were being recruited prior to finishing their education for the priesthood on the Continent, no candidate with the surname of Mullowney would be accepted.

The preparatory schools were damp caves and similar hideouts. Those were the Penal Days in Ireland when, in the words of the old poem,

> They bribed the flock; they bribed the son,
> To sell the priest, to rob the sire,
> Their dogs were taught alike to run,
> Upon the scent of wolf and friar.

England's Penal Laws against Irish Catholics got into their stride at the close of the seventeenth century. They grew progressively more severe over the entire eighteenth century. The sums of bribe money paid in this persecution ranged from £100 for the apprehension or death of an archbishop or bishop down to £10 for a friar.

It was said that the Irish clerical students could be easily recognised when they got to the Continent by their red eyes and the smell of turf smoke. Living and studying in damp caves, a good turf fire was needed, regardless of other effects. The fires at night had to be extinguished during the day so no tell-tale smoke would give the spies a clue. The owners of the boats that took students to the Continent were usually smugglers, who abounded on the west coast of Ireland in those days.

Running the gauntlet of the English navy and the elements, they probably had no more than an even chance of reaching the mainland of Europe in their light luggers, as their small boats were called. The smugglers were the unsung heroes who would help to keep the people's hopes alive in dark and evil days.

The ordained priests were taken aback by the fact that the 'smokers' faced certain deaths if they were caught in Ireland or, as often happened, on the high seas. In these cases, the smuggler and his crew shared the same fate, with their ultimate end unknown and unre-

corded. The Oath of Abjuration introduced in 1712 stipulated that all Roman Catholic clergymen who did not swear to abjure all Roman Catholic practices and rituals by a certain date were to be transported, and any who returned again would have rendered his life forfeit to the Crown. Out of nearly 2,000 Roman Catholic clergymen of all ranks, only thirty-three, all in poor health, took the oath. The only Mayo clergyman to take the oath was named as Father John Durkin of Killedan parish.

Later in the same year, the Protestant archbishop of Tuam, Archbishop Vesey, convened a meeting of priest-hunters from all over Ireland for what today would be termed a pep talk. It was said that he changed his religion and his way of life when he was arrested on a charge of horse stealing and sentenced to death. He was pardoned when he agreed to change his religion and become a priest-hunter.

He is believed to have been given a post of responsibility in this fight for the 'Cause'. From that time on, he covered the whole of Connacht, accompanied by a posse of soldiers to protect and assist him in his priest-hunting activities.

Prior to this, his patron and paymaster was Bingham of Newbrook, Claremorris. This Bingham was Lord Clanmorris while the Castlebar Bingham was Lord Lucan.

Both worthies were kinsmen and were equally oppressive in their attitudes to the plain people. The Brownes who succeeded the Binghams carried on in the same tradition. Shaun Mullowney is believed to have been born in a townland, Skehanagh, 5 or 6 miles from Castlebar around the year 1680. He was born in a turbulent part of County Mayo, an area that had been unsettled for centuries.

One of my informants said the good limestone land there was worth fighting for. The nearby castle of Kinturk with its projecting hanging stone was a place where rough justice was dispensed for centuries by the warlike Stauntons. In 1388, Edmund de Burgo (Burke), a son of the Red Earl, was drowned in Lough Mask with a stone around his neck.

For their part or suspected part in his murder, the powerful de Burgo exacted a heavy revenge on the Stauntons. One sept of the Stuantons to escape the de Burgo vendetta changed their surname to Mac Evilly. This surname, formerly pronounced 'Mac Aveeley', is found in the Castlebar area.

Archbishop Mac Aveeley was a successor to Archbishop McHale in the See of Tuam. He is chiefly remembered for his long reign. Captain Seamas McEvilly was one of the Castlebar IRA men who died fighting the Black and Tans at Kilmeena in the long hot summer of 1921. Shaun Mullowney was described as being powerfully built and athletic, with low cunning and intuition to suit his nefarious occupation.

For a long time, he seems to have lead a charmed life. When his arch-enemy, Fergus McCormack, who fought at Aughrim as a youth and was known as the Rapparee, and others planned ambushes for him, he changed routes and plans at the last minute.

Shaun Mullowney's first murder of a priest is believed to have been that of Father Higgins at the cave of Pollathackeen on the West Mayo coast. The priest was saying Mass when Mullowney surprised him. He had almost escaped in a boat when Mullowney plunged waist deep into the water and shot him.

Around 1724, a young curate, Fr David Burke, had arranged to celebrate Mass in the granary on the Lane in Castlebar. Castlebar at that time was described as containing a maze of lanes.

It was a big market day in the town and the priest, in disguise, had been acting as an assistant to a packman or second-hand clothes dealer at his stall on the market square. The man, known as Johnny McCann, was deeply distrusted by the priest-hunter.

Mullowney had a close watch kept on him in his stall. When the time came to celebrate Mass, McCann's assistant slipped away silently. The direction he took was noted by Mullowney, who followed slowly behind him. He saw one or two entering the granary, which was filled to the door with people. A lookout shouted 'Shaun na Soggarth!' several times. The crowd upstairs in the granary panicked and rushed for the door. In their mad rush, the rotten floor of the granary collapsed and one feeble old man was crushed to death. The priest hastily stowed his sacred vessels inside his coat and jumped out the window, where he was grabbed by the wily Mullowney, who had been expecting this.

As Mullowney pinned the priest down, some of the crowd pulled the priest-hunter's long overcoat over his head and loosened his grip on his adversary, who lost no time in getting out of the town.

Hearing from the spies of Lord Lucan that a priest named Fr Kilger had come back, Mullowney swore that he would not rest until he had the priest at the end of his dagger.

Mullowney had been responsible for having this priest transported to the Continent some years before this. When all his plans and inquiries failed to bring any success, he decided to use his sister, a widow named Nancy Loughnan, as a pawn to achieve his blood-thirsty ambition. One cold, wet evening, he stumbled into his sister's in Ballyheane.

Feigning a wracking cough and weakness, he asked to be allowed to stay the night. On the following day, he said he was much worse. His sister, a devout Catholic, who detested Shaun and his actions, eventually showed an interest in his condition. Seeing this, Shaun professed repentance for his past life and said he would die happy if he could only confess his sins to the man he had wronged so much, Fr Kilger.

Falling for this agonised plea, she went to the house of one of her neighbours, where she knew she would find both Fr Kilger and his nephew, Fr Burke. Returning with Fr Kilger, she waited outside the door as the priest entered. Hearing shouts and the sounds of a struggle, Nancy entered the house and met Shaun rushing out with his bloodstained dagger. He ran across the fields towards Castlebar. Father Kilger lay dying on the floor in a pool of blood. The widow fainted with shock.

When she recovered, she crept back to the house she had visited. There she told her story and fainted again. Father Burke refused to heed her advice to flee and said he would attend the funeral and bless his uncle's grave. The funeral was hastily arranged for the following morning to hoodwink the authorities. Nevertheless, John Bingham had sent out a troop of soldiers to frighten the peasantry.

After the funeral had covered a mile or more of the road to Ballintubber, Shaun na Soggarth, who was concealed behind a whitethorn hedge, leaped out onto the road and grabbed Fr Burke, who was disguised in a long peasant's frieze coat. The priest managed to struggle free, leap over the roadside fence and run away in the direction of the Partry Hills. The epic chase with Mullowney is still remembered to this day, almost 300 years later.

The chase, which ended in Partry, covered several townlands and took a circuitous route through Derridaffderg and Shraigh. The whole concourse, including soldiers, stood and watched until the chase disappeared from view. They had possibly thought the priest-hunter would be happier to kill or take back his quarry singlehandedly.

The spectators saw another man suddenly joining the race and he began closing on the other pair. When the chase got to Partry, Fr Burke, in desperation, suddenly swung around and grappled with Mullowney. As both rolled on the ground, he wounded Shaun in the arm with a dagger thrust. The third runner came up just then and lost no time in plunging his dagger into Mullowney's side. Mullowney was able to identify him as Johnny McCann.

To rub salt into a dying priest-hunter's wounds, the packman told him that his name was not McCann but Higgins. 'I am a nephew of the man you murdered at Pollathackeen. I have longed and waited for the day I would avenge my uncle's death.'

Ironically, Shaun na Soggarth was buried in the cemetery of Ballintubber Abbey. A withered ash tree marks the grave where he lies. A plain stone near Partry garda station is said to mark the spot where he met his death.

The two men involved in the death of Shaun na Soggarth escaped the manhunt that followed. In a party that included Mullowney's sister and McCormack the Rapparee, they were believed to have escaped to France later.

I got much of this information from an aunt who lived in Gary, Indiana, over fifty years ago. She had the advantage of reading in her youth *A Life of Shaun na Soggarth*, written by a Castlebar writer Anthony Archdeacon. Unfortunately, the book has long been unobtainable.

33

THE WELSHMEN
OF TIRAWLEY

The early Norman invasion or invasions of Ireland in the late twelfth and early thirteenth centuries were not strictly confined to Norman adventurers. While the better armed, mail-clad Normans may be regarded as the shock troops that took all the choicest spoils of conquest, a goodly number of Welsh and Anglo-Normans were also involved.

The Welsh adventurers were the first fortune hunters of that era to come to County Mayo. The Normans who came later to take the lion's share of the plunder pushed them westward. The Normans included the De Burgos who later became the Burkes and the De Exeters, who later changed their name to Mac Jordan, later again dropping the Gaelic prefix, 'Mac'.

The D'Angulos did the same after changing their name to Mac Costello, while some of the Claremorris De Prendergasts changed their name to Mac Morris.

Tirawley, the North Mayo barony, seems to have been the happy hunting ground of the Welshmen while the going was good. Cusacks, Barrets, Lynotts, Flemings and Evans are all names considered to be being of Welsh origin.

In 1281, almost 100 years after the first Norman invasion, a fierce battle in which scores were killed was fought at Kilroe, beside Killalla. This battle was unusual as the main contenders were Welsh factions, the Barrets and the Cusacks. The Barrets and the Flemirigs were overcome by the Cusacks, who were aided by the local Gaelic chief, Torlach O'Dubhda (O'Dowd).

O'Dowd was killed by the Cusacks on a North Sligo strand some months later. It seems that alliances were short-lived in those days, but to quote a latter-day phrase, 'there was never a dull moment'. A better-remembered clash between Welshmen occurred in 1394, involving the Barrets and the Lynotts in the Crossmolina area. The Barrets at that time were overlords of the Barony of Tirawley and tried to exact tribute from, among others, the Lynotts. A poet of the last century, Samuel Ferguson, in the opening lines of his epic poem 'The Welshmen of Tirawley', gives the reason for the historic blood feud between the Lynotts and the Barrets:

> Scorna Boy (Buidhe) the Barrets' bailiff, lewd and lame,
> With evil thoughts and threats and writs
> Unto the Lynotts came.
> When he rudely drew a young maid to him,
> Then the Lynotts rose and slew him
> And in Tubber na Scorna threw him.

In retaliation, the numerically superior Barrets seized a dozen of the fighting men of the Lynotts. They offered them a grim choice: either to lose their manhood or their eyes. Having opted to lose their eyes, the Lynotts were taken to a spot where a line of stepping stones crossed the Dubhowen or Black River. Any Lynott who crossed the river in a stumbling, slipping way got his freedom but any who walked across without faltering got another blinding. But in spite of all the precautions, at least one victim got away with only minor injuries to his eyes. This was Edmond Lynott of Garranard (*Garán an Ard*).

As the Lynotts were on good terms with the De Burgos (Burkes), they soon sought them out for their sympathy. Six years previously, Richard De Burgo of Carra had got a grant, on paper, of all Connacht from the King of England, in return for an annuity of 500 marks and ten knights. The De Burgos, despite some setbacks and interruptions, were able to enforce their claim up to the Flight of the Earls in the early seventeenth century. The ancient system of fosterage was in vogue at the time of the Barret/Lynott confrontation and the Lynotts had adopted in fosterage a son of Edmond Burke of Castlebar. As hostilities worsened, the Barrets killed this foster son of Lynott at the ford of Cornasack on the Crossmolina/ Ballycastle road.

According to Duald Mac Firbis, the last of the great family of analysts and genealogists, the decline of the Barret power and the rise of the De Burgos as rulers of Tirawley date to this event. Incidentally, in later times, Mac Firbis was murdered at the Inn of Doonflynn in North Sligo, between Templeboy and Skreen. He was said to have been on his way to a gathering of writers and analysts in Dublin. He was trying to save a lady from being molested by a drunken patron of the inn at the time.

Local tradition holds that with the intervention of the De Burgos in the Welshmen of Tirawley feud, the branch of the Barret clan directly involved were forced to retreat to the uncharted wastes of Erris, where they changed their name to Mac Andrew. This name is a popular surname in Mayo today.

Strangely, the surname of Cusack is rarely met, despite the Cusacks being the ruling faction in Tirawley at one time and the area around Killala being known as 'Cusack's Country'. The well to which the Lynotts consigned Scorna Boy Barret was afterwards called 'Tubber na Scorna' (Scorna's Well), while the stepping stones utilised for the Barret eye-testing scheme were afterwards called *Clocháin na nDall* (the stepping stones of the blind).

34

LEG WARMERS
AND *TREHEENS*

S ome time ago, a relative told me of a purchase which she had recently made with which she was very pleased. This was a pair of sole-less stockings known as leg warmers. She said they were wonderful value and wondered that such a useful invention had not been thought of earlier. She seemed more than surprised that her invention, under the name of *treheens*, had been known to her ancestors for possibly thousands of years.

The light-footed, lightly armed Irish soldiers known as Kerna sported sole-less hosiery, which were of course *treheens*, and in severe weather they were said to wear wooden-soled sandals, secured to the legs with rawhide thongs. Some sketches suggest that only a plain wooden sole was used in many cases.

As late as 200 years ago, a tough, hard-drinking fraternity from Northern Ireland came to Connacht for cock-fighting matches, mostly held in the winter months. To emphasise their toughness, they came on horseback wearing *treheens* and when there was snow on the ground, they carried a handful of straw, which they put under their feet when they dismounted. They called themselves 'The Devil's Fliers'.

Word got around that some of them were English officers in disguise from the garrison at Enniskillen and as they were believed to carry concealed weapons, they mostly got their way.

In my younger days, I heard an old Donegal *seanchaí* describe a battle fought around 1647, the Battle of Scarrifhollis (*Scaribh Salach*).

This battle is rarely mentioned in Irish history despite being a decisive, bloody engagement, which finished the Catholic cause in Ulster at the time. According to the *seanchaí*, the Catholic force was a formidable one, containing three crack regiments that were previously part of Owen Roe's army. In addition, the infantry contained hundreds of battle-hardened veterans who had fought with Owen Roe in the Low Countries.

A good many of the infantry were local recruits with hastily fashioned pikes and as they wore *treheens* they might as well have been barefooted, as the *seanchaí* aptly said. For some reason, the Donegal bishop, Heber McMahon, insisted on leading the Irish army. When he decided on an immediate attack on the Puritan Covenanter army, some veteran army officers tried to dissuade him.

They pointed out that the boulder-strewn terrain was highly unsuitable for cavalry manoeuvres and that the thorn bushes and briars would make matters worse for both the cavalry and that section of the infantry wearing *treheens*. Against all advice, the fiery bishop decided to attack, with disastrous results. The Irish army was heavily defeated and Bishop McMahon was captured and executed in a barbarous manner.

Digressing at this point, I may mention that in our lopsided presentation of history nearly every Irish schoolchild is taught about the victories of Clontarf, Benburb, the Yellow Ford, the Curlew Mountains or the Races of Castlebar – some of them pyrrhic victories.

Decisive battles like Scariffhollis or Dungan's Hill, near Trim in 1647, are rarely mentioned. Dungan's Hill ended the Catholic Confederate cause in Leinster and was rated the bloodiest battle fought in that province. (Preston's army was defeated by the Puritan army under Jones.)

Similarly, the Battle of Knocknanoss, near Kinsale in County Cork, is seldom mentioned. This battle was also fought in 1647 and ended Catholic resistance in Munster. The Catholic leader, Lord Taafe of Ballymote, stood idly by and allowed 1,200 Scottish Redshanks to be wiped out by the victorious Inchiquin (Morrogh the Burner).

The legendary Alastrom McDonnell died with his Scots comrades, who fought almost to the last man. It should be noted in relation to this war that what was referred to as the Catholic cause, was in reality the Catholic landowners' cause.

I was told in my younger days about a visit by my great-grandmother to a blessed well in Balla (and then on to climb Croaghpatrick) around the famine years. She felt that the children were old enough and wise enough to look after themselves and she wanted to pay a long-promised visit to the blessed well.

So she set off, taking two pairs of newly knitted *treheens* and a pair of high-buttoned boots that were to be worn only in an emergency. Sometime after she left home, there was a general rush to enjoy a pot of tea, and she had been very strict and sparing in the use of that commodity.

Tea was then a rare item, only recently introduced to the area. The teapot, often borrowed by neighbours for tea-making experiments, was a tin one, made by an itinerant tinsmith. The spout was so long and thin that my great-grandmother used to say that she could almost stand by the fire and pour out a mug of tea on the table.

The revellers that my great-grandmother left behind were in a state of panic when they could not find the lid of the teapot. They had to use a slice of turnip, a crop only recently introduced to the area.

When their mother was doing her penitential walk in the ancient cemetery beside the blessed well in Balla, she stood on a broken bottle, cutting her foot. This meant that she had to wear her high-buttoned boots. When she unbuttoned her boots, out rolled the teapot lid from one of them. 'Oh, well,' she said, 'that will stop the tea making at home until I get back.' In this, she was slightly off the mark!

It has been said that the pilgrimage in Balla in those days could attract up to 20,000 pilgrims. I have a recollection of hearing two old men at a fair in Balla engaging in an argument in a pub. 'My ancestors,' said one, 'were able to go to the Fair of Brize in shoes and stockings when yours could only go to the pattern in Balla wearing *treheens!*'

Patterns, it should be noted, were gatherings originally intended to commemorate some local saint (of the old Celtic Church) or other notable. Athletic games, sports and fairs got on the agenda and often there was the inevitable fight to round off the proceedings.

In a doggerel poem by a local poet deriding the imposition of a dog tax by the British government early in the twentieth century, the *treheen* is mentioned:

> Poor Pat is in the bog,
> With a treheen in his clog
> And five shillings for his dog,
> Said the grand old man.

The government, having previously granted pensions of five shillings weekly to people over 70 years of age, recouped themselves with a dog tax of £5 annually, as dogs considerably outnumbered pensioners.

I recollect seeing a woman of over 90 in a remote area of Mayo in 1942 wearing *treheens* (and no footwear) on a cold November evening. She was living alone and was taking in a basket of turf for the fire. She was known locally as Old Peggy. When I congratulated her on her health and hardiness she drew herself up proudly and said, 'I would not swap my *treheens* with the Queen of England.'

I thought for a moment of how the spirit of Old Peggy (Lyncheaun) epitomised the uncompromising spirit of the Gael over 1,000 years of Dane, Norman and English presence.

35

WHEN THE MOTOR
CAR CAME WEST

Many tales, grave and gay, true and false, are still remembered in relation to the coming of the first motor cars to the west of Ireland, around the beginning of the twentieth century. It is believed by many Mayo people that the first private car to come to Mayo was purchased by Sir Henry Lynch-Blosse of Athavallie House, Balla. This house was later taken over by the Sisters of Mercy and is now a secondary school.

He purchased his car in Dublin and had it sent to Balla railway station, well wrapped and packed in canvas wrappings. It was taken from there to his nearby mansion by railway float. A few days later, as arranged, a driver for the car arrived by rail from Dublin. He was well equipped with dust goggles and a driver's cap with high, pointed earflaps that could be folded down over the ears in stormy or frosty weather. The cars in those early motoring days had no fixed roofs. A folding canvas roof with celluloid squares to act as windows was used until the all-weather cars came along some years later.

Next day, after the arrival of the chauffeur, Sir Henry decided to give the car its maiden run – to Claremorris, if all went well. The driver, accompanied by Sir Henry, took the car onto the main Castlebar–Balla road and then turned east towards Balla.

Rounding the bend near the Glebe, or parson's house, they saw a well-known knight of the road 40 or 50 yards ahead and travelling in the same direction. He was known locally as *Seán Bacach*. Hearing the loud rumbling noise behind him *Seán* looked around and came to a standstill in the centre of the road. He almost dropped with fright. The car slowed down but two or three blasts from the horn, or hooter, caused Seán to run ahead at top speed. Even though he always boasted of being 'as light in foot as a Tyrone ragman', he found that the monster was gaining on him. His first impression was that he was seeing the headless coach of prophecy and legend, complete with the Evil One, who was abducting Sir Henry and probably taking him to warmer regions.

As Seán had heard many fireside tales on such themes, he felt that legend was being translated into reality before his eyes. In his fleeting backward glance, the high pointed cap of the driver registered as the devil's horns and the goggles confirmed his worst conclusions.

Coming to a small bridge or gullet beside the modern Woodlands housing estate, he flung himself over the parapet wall and crept well under the eye of the bridge. He found that the stream was completely dried up, as always in prolonged dry weather

When the fugitive plucked up the courage to peep out from under the bridge, he was horrified to see the headless coach and its occupants at a standstill at the crossroad 100 yards ahead. A well-known blacksmith's forge, Keville's, stood at this crossroads. This gave Seán a faint glimmer of hope.

Blacksmiths in those days were credited with occult powers above the ordinary, especially where evil spirits were involved. Seán thought that the blacksmith might have invoked some charm to halt the devil in his tracks. He said a silent prayer that the blacksmith would be able to turn the anvil on the devil and banish him off with a few well-chosen potent curses.

However, to Seán's disappointment, the headless coach and its occupants turned slowly towards Balla.

Seán then jumped into the wood and, dodging between the trees, he got to the Parochial House, where he told the parish priest his story. On his way through the wood, he judged, by the trail of fire and smoke at the devil's rear, that he had gone out the Claremorris road between the two fair greens. The 'smoke' that Seán saw was probably dust. (The use of tar in later years to keep down dust was one of the great innovations of those days.) Seán burst into his story to the parish priest in a half-hysterical manner.

He described the devil's eyes, 'twice as big as cow's eyes', and his horns short and sharp. He described the terrifying roars of the devil (the rubber-ball type horn emitted an ear-shattering roar when squeezed). Seán could be excused for coupling those bloodcurdling roars with His Satanic Majesty. The parish priest had a good idea as to what Seán had really seen, as he had advance news of the intended purchase of the car from Sir Harry. To allay Seán's fears, the parish priest said that if Sir Harry did not return in a few hours, he would see what could be done about it.

'A few hours!' exclaimed Seán, aghast. 'At the rate they went out the Rathduff road, they will be in Hell in half the time. If you can do no good by prayers or curses, you could send a *tallywagger* (telegram) to the peelers in Claremorris or Dublin to stop him.'

'Well,' replied the parish priest, 'if you agree to leave everything in my hands, I will promise that everything will turn out alright.'

So Seán agreed to call off his demon hunt.

A West of Ireland bishop of those days also purchased a new motor car. The name of his particular purchase was the 'Moon'. A brother of the bishop was one of the local town 'gods', a bunch of cynics who used to meet daily at a certain street corner to engage in criticism, both constructive and destructive, of the changing times and of innovations and events in general.

On one occasion, when the bishop's brother saw the 'Moon' approaching, he said to his companions, 'You were talking a few minutes ago about the changing times and there is one of the biggest changes of all before our eyes. We read in the Bible about Our Lord riding on His ass and now here comes our "Tomeen" riding on the moon!'

I heard a story in Achill relating to those early motoring days. While the story in general may be true, there are parts that can be taken with the proverbial grain of salt.

A young Achill man emigrated to Cleveland, USA, during the closing years of the nineteenth century. After a few successful years in the saloon business, he decided to come back to visit the old home and also to take one of his nephews back to Cleveland with him. He decided to surprise his relatives by taking a car with him from

Dublin. Owing to the poor roads and slow travelling speeds of those days, that meant staying a night in Athlone.

His relations in the home place had a few busy days giving a facelift to the buildings and surroundings. The empty farmyard manure pit was regarded as an eyesore and a covering of fresh hay was spread over it for camouflage. When the Yank arrived, he drove up on the hay and promptly got stuck there. A neighbour, known as Pat Vicky, had a mule so strong that, in Pat's words, 'he did not know his own strength'. The mule was brought out and it pulled the car onto terra firma. When the car owner told Pat some days later that the car was ten horsepower, Pat replied that his mule must be eleven or twelve horsepower considering he was able to do what ten horses failed to do.

On the day after his arrival, the Yank proposed a trip around the island and out to Mulranny by car. The only one to venture with him was the nephew he hoped to take to America. A tree growing in front of the house was a partial obstruction, so they had to drive by slowly in order to get onto the main road.

When they got to the main road, they kept to a steady 20mph owing to the poor condition of the sand roads of those days. When they left the island, they went through Currane to Mulranny and returned through Tonragee. When they got back home, the Yank did not allow for the slippery, greasy state of the byroad and slammed on the brakes too sharply, with the result that the car skidded into the tree in front of the house. As the roof was folded back, driver and nephew were pitched out on their hands and knees, without injury.

'Well,' exclaimed the nephew, 'you did well to stop it that time, Uncle, but what would you do if there was no tree?'

36

In the Year of the Hot Summer

U ntil recent years, 1921 was often referred to in the west of Ireland as the year of the hot summer. Some shorter heat-waves in that year were followed by a record-breaking spell of hot, dry weather extending from mid-May to mid-July.

The armed struggle with the British forces occupying Ireland – military, RIC and Black and Tans – had reached its peak, ending with a truce that took effect on 11 July 1921.

In the warfare preceding the truce, that IRA had no course open to them but guerrilla tactics.

They were outnumbered, possibly to the tune of twenty to one, by an enemy infinitely better armed and equipped, so their only hope lay in what Lloyd George called the 'hit and run strategy'.

The fine summer weather enabled active service IRA units to sleep in the open, often under clumps of *whins* (furze) or *sally* (willow) bushes to escape detection by spotter planes. West Mayo was one of the busy theatres of war.

I worked as a supervisor on the construction of mountain and bog roads, bridges and boat 'slips' or small piers in the Westport area, sometime after the outbreak of the Second World War. On one occasion, I had an interesting conversation with an old man in McKeon's public house in Drummin. We talked of the Troubled Times.

'You know,' he said, 'that the Westport area was always a busy spot, even going back to 1916.'

He told me that martial law was declared for Westport and the surrounding area in 1920. Anyone entering or leaving the town could be arrested and jailed if they did not have a permit from the RIC or some British authority.

The Americans sent over three leading Irish-American lawyers and politicians, Walsh, Ryan and Dunne, to tour Ireland and get all the facts about the Black and Tans and the reign of terror then prevailing in Ireland.

The British government did not interfere until the emissaries approached Westport. There they were met at Knappagh on the Leenane road and were turned back in typical imperialist style with no explanation by an armoured car squad. This shows how well the British were keeping an eye on Westport. The real troubles did not reach this quiet countryside area until early in 1921.

'One moonlit night,' continued my informant, 'Michael Kilroy of Newport, the OC of the West Mayo brigade of the IRA, was cycling around here with four or five of his officers. He was supposed to be picking a suitable ambush spot. Around the bend down there on the road they came face to face with a scouting party of the RIC that was also cycling. The IRA order to take cover and fire was rapidly obeyed and that short, sharp encounter ended with Sergeant Coughlan dead and police constables McGuire, Love and Creedon wounded and disarmed. From that time until the truce, we did not get much ease or peace from the authorities around here.'

Just across the valley from Drummin, lies the bleak, stony village of Carrowkennedy, which was the scene of one of the fiercest encounters of the old days between the IRA and the British forces.

My immediate superior on the local county council supervisory staff was a man who played a leading role in the Carrowkennedy encounter and other major engagements leading up to it. His family was deeply involved in the struggle for freedom and his forefathers had been involved in the national and anti-landlord activities down through the years.

As he is, I hope, still going strong and of a most unassuming disposition, I will not use his surname but will refer to him by his first name of Johnny.

'You know,' he said, 'our successful action at Carrowkennedy was long overdue. Up to two or three months previously, we had undergone a period of hard training under our brigadier, Michael Kilroy, who left nothing half done. Then we met two setbacks which only served to make us redouble our efforts and take no one necessary risks.

'In one of those reverses, the whole force of RIC and Tans from Westport set out to encircle and surprise us in a night attack on Skirdagh, below Newport. The surprise attempt was foiled by our sentries and resulted in a 15-hour fight in which a plane and strong reinforcements were called on to assist the Newport RIC and Tans. Our better knowledge helped us to get outside the enemy cordon at night. On 19 May, we suffered an ugly reverse at Kilmeena, between Westport and Newport. It was one of those happenings when the best-laid plans can all go wrong at the last moment.

'A routine enemy convoy travelling along the Westport–Newport road was to be attacked at Knocknaboly. A larger, better-armed enemy convoy than expected came along earlier than anticipated. As this early arrival had not been expected, many of the IRA men had not arrived or got into position.

'To make matters worse, the first carload of RIC was preceded by a carload of nuns in their black uniforms. A lookout man mistook the dark-uniformed RIC for a second carload of nuns and did not act to stop them until it was too late.

'When the two lorry loads of Tans arrived, they were immediately attacked by the IRA. The RIC car, mistakenly allowed through, returned and opened fire on the IRA with a machine gun from the high ground at the bridge. To make matters worse, a second machine gun opened fire on the IRA from the opposite side of the road.

'Two thirds of the IRA just had shotguns, which were only useful at short range or when an element of surprise was involved.

'The OC ordered a retreat and fought a rearguard action with his riflemen. In that action, his coolness and good marksmanship went a long way towards getting the column out of an ugly situation. On 2 July 1921, two weeks after the unlucky reverse at Kilmeena, we came to grips with the ancient enemy again at Carrowkennedy.'

After a reflective pause, Johnny began again. 'On that day, three lorry loads of Tans and a carload of RIC arrived in the early afternoon from Westport and halted in Carrowkennedy. Here, the road had been cut across and they commandeered a number of turf workers with their loads of turf and compelled them to fill in the trench on the road with the turf and then they drove on to Connemara.

'We arrived at Carrowkennedy after the enemy's departure and we set to work making peep holes for our rifles in the stone walls and altering some stones to a higher level.

'We were just finishing our work when we got the word that the Tans were back and were at Darby's pub. When the leading lorry came opposite us, it received a full volley and crashed into the wall.

'The driver, Police Inspector Stevenson, was shot dead. Two of the Tans jumped out. One of them was discovered under a bank, shivering with fright when the fight was over. The man had not fired a single shot. The other Tan was lying prone with his gun, as I thought, pointing straight at my loophole in the wall. I had kept banging away at him with no visible results.

'After the fight I went over to him and found that his head was simply scalped by my bullets and I concluded that the man might have been dead after my first shot.

'Well, war is war and my only regret at the time was for all the valuable ammunition I had wasted. The Tans in the first lorry had a machine gun and immediately opened up on our position. One of our snipers shot the gunner and two others who followed met a similar fate. The gunner, of course, had to expose himself more than the riflemen. As the fight was going on for too long for our wishes, the OC said we had neither the time nor the ammunition to continue in this way and we'd have to get in closer to rush the lorry. Jack Keane, my brother and I were picked to get closer to the lorry on our side of the road.

'Joe Baker, Tom Ainsworth and Hagan were picked to creep closer on the other side of the road. Jack McDonagh and Tom Heavey were to cover up for us as we edged closer to the enemy.

'We hoped that we might be able to lob in one or two of our homemade bombs, which, with luck, might explode and in the confusion we would be able to rush the lorry. As we moved closer, a Tan on the point of firing a rifle grenade was shot and the grenade fell into the lorry, killing two policemen. The rest hoisted a white flag. All the RIC and Tans in that lorry were either killed or wounded, except the one under the bank who had jumped out. The other two lorry loads of Tans had still to be dealt with.'

After the first shots they had abandoned their lorries and rushed to the house of the Widow McGreal. In their hurry, they had left a keg of rifle ammunition behind in the lorry and tried to induce the widow to order her young son to go out and retrieve it. She scornfully told them to do their own dirty work if they were brave enough.

'They had plenty of rifle grenades but the range to our positions was too long. Still, they ignored all calls to surrender. Luckily, one of our men, Jamie Flaherty from Westport, had been an army machine gun operator in Flanders three or four years previously. We soon set up our captured machine gun and trained it on the house. At the first burst of fire, he cut the door to ribbons and then he trained it on the thatch of the roof, which he sent flying in waves.

'Knowing that the sparks flying from the stonework would soon set the thatch on fire, the occupants pushed the dish towel out the window and surrendered. The coolest occupant of the house was the widow herself, who laughed and joked and hoped we had killed all the black devils. The Tans expected death after their record of tortures and reprisals, but Michael Kilroy turned down any suggestions in that regard. The injured had their wounds dressed and he gave one RIC man a pass to be allowed through the IRA sentries so he could get medical attention for the wounded in Westport.

'He also warned him that any reprisals would be drastically dealt with. Then the booty was collected and the vehicles were set on fire. Some of the boys almost wept for joy,' said Johnny, 'when they handled the machine gun that had turned the tables on them at Kilmeena two weeks earlier.

'We found that we had taken thirty rifles and about the same number of revolvers and, most prized of all, apart from the machine gun, 5,000 rounds of .303 rifle ammunition. Before the fight, Kilroy was asked what his line of retreat would be and he replied that it would be to Aughagower, through Sraheen.

'When we moved off from Carrowkennedy, the OC gave us the order to march down the road to Sraheen. After going a short distance, he stopped to talk to a local man, Sonny O'Malley. He then gave us the right wheel command doubling us back on our tracks over the Leenane-Westport road and on to the hills behind Croaghpatrick.

'He had told O'Malley to inform any enemy search parties that he had seen us marching down the Sraheen road in military formation, which was of course true. O'Malley carried out those instructions and was thanked by a British officer for his help!

'Sometime later, as we were resting at the top of Maum a' Chassagh and were watching the enemy plane cruising and diving over Aughagower, we felt more inclined than ever to trust in our leader's foresight and coolness. The Joyces of Durless, Black Pat and Red Pat gave us a royal welcome and killed a sheep to entertain us. I think I have tasted no mutton so sweet from that day to this.

'Later, our men spent a few days around the Creggans and Ailmore, where the people were wonderfully kind and hospitable to them but they felt the need to move on because, with the sea at their backs, they were in a restricted area if the need for a quick getaway arose. After the ambush at Carrowkennedy, the rumour had gone out that the IRA unit had gone to Tourmakeady to link up with the South Mayo battalion. Sometime before the action at Carrowkennedy, a large-scale engagement took place at Tourmakeady, where Tom Maguire and his South Mayo men took on an enemy force there. After losses of four or five men killed and some more wounded, the RIC and Tans withdrew.

'They returned after 2 hours with huge reinforcements and after making contact with the IRA, a huge engagement took place, lasting until darkness fell. A factor that gave a temporary respite to the IRA on that occasion was the fact that the British army reinforcements from Clarermorris, advancing up the Partry Hills, shot at more troops from Castlebar, who were coming over the hills from the western side.

'As there was a slight fog or haze hanging over the hilltops, they mistook the Castlebar troops for the West Mayo IRA coming to the assistance of their South Mayo comrades and opened fire on them. An undisclosed number was killed and more were wounded before the mistake was discovered. The authorities were to go to great lengths to hush up the whole affair, even dispatching coffins by rail from Ballinrobe station in sealed and darkened carriages.

'On that day the IRA OC, Tom Maguire, was wounded, suffering a broken arm. His adjutant, Michael O'Brien, was shot dead while assisting him to bandage his wound. Tom Maguire, though suffering intense pain, went back and continued to direct operations until nightfall when the column got outside enemy lines. Tales of the subsequent escape of Tom Maguire and his men during the intensive comb-out of the area by thousands of British troops are legendary.

'On the day of the Tourmakeady fight, Michael Kilroy got the message that the South Mayo men were surrounded in Partry. Kilroy and his men were then at the foot of Buckagh mountain north of Westport. He set off with a cycling column and they travelled all through the night. When they got to Glenmask, they learned that the men from South Mayo were safe.'

Believing the rumour that Mick Kilroy and his men had gone to the Partry–Tourmakeady region after Carrowkennedy to link up with the units in South Mayo, a second comb-out of the area by the British forces took place. Finding nobody home, they returned to the search in West Mayo. Strangely enough, they kept on the trail of the 'boys' right up to the truce and never seemed to be more than a day or two behind. Indeed, they often arrived only an hour or two after the IRA had moved on.

The IRA trail led from Aughagower to Islandeady, Glenhest, the glens around Nephin and on to Tavanaghmore and Ballyclogher. It was decided at this time to divide the column into sections.

With more than 3,000 troops on their trail, along with planes and even cavalry squads to search mountain areas, an unwieldy column of fifty men stood little chance of survival, even though they were better armed than ever before.

Owing to the continuing fine weather, the enemy adopted the IRA tactics of sleeping out in the open or in bell tents that could be set up in a matter of minutes.

The IRA men's luck continued after the splitting up of the column up to the truce ten days later. Two days after the truce, a heavy shower of rain heralded a break in the record-breaking hot summer.

37

BEFORE SCHOOL BUSES

Watching a queue of school boys and girls boarding a homeward bus recently reminded me of my school days. In addition to the amount of bottles of soft drinks, potato crisps, candies and chocolate taken on board, there was also a number of light magazines of little or no educational value. I saw one youngster who dropped a halfpenny from his hands full of change look down disdainfully on the ha'penny. He did not even stoop to pick it up.

In my school days, Pat Moran and his wife, Mary Flynn, kept a neat, well-stocked shop in Swinford, where sweets, fruit and many smaller grocery items were stocked. The most prized items of all were Pat Moran's handfuls of sweets, a peculiar measurement that amounted to whatever came up in his hand when he plunged it into a shining can of 'bullseyes'. Mary Flynn's handful was only a small pinch compared to Pat's straight handful.

I often saw tempers raised and small fists flying in defence of Pat or Mary when it came to deciding the relative merits of either's 'ha'porth' of sweets. I may add that halfpennies were so scarce that the ones who were in a position to buy sweets had to share them around or were liable to have them hijacked.

The First World War and cruel inflation put an end to ha'porths of sweets. Against the heaps of goodies enjoyed by modern schoolchildren, we had to make do with berries sweet or sour (mostly sour), sloes, crab apples, hips and haws, blackberries and wild raspberries.

All those items had to be consumed by November Night, when we were told they would be polluted by the *Púca* (Pooka).

A feed of raw turnips was considered a luxury, especially if the turnips had been sweetened by frost. Often, we were chased by irate farmers when they felt we overdid our visits to their turnip fields.

One of the most dreaded hazards for schoolchildren in my school-going days was meeting a cross gander.

Most of the small farms in those days had a flock of geese, complete with ganders, to help out the farm economy. Those birds were not handfed, except at Christmas when they were being fattened with small waste potatoes and fistfuls of inferior grain. This left the gander in fighting condition in our estimation. A half-starved gander was an adversary to be avoided and feared by young school children.

Any child who got bitten by a gander or got slashed by his powerful wings would thereafter give him a wide berth. Those birds were regarded as polluters of pastures and many flocks were maintained along the roadside by their owners' holdings.

Around 1920, speeding Black and Tans loved to drive through those flocks of geese, leaving a trail of death and destruction in their wake, and they were also liable to take potshots at the geese for good measure. This, coupled with ever-increasing road traffic, led to these flocks being taken off the roads.

One legendary gander was owned by a widow who lived in a quiet spot by the River Moy. This bird was reputedly over 20 years old and if it had not been for the fact that he met a sticky end he would undoubtedly have clocked up a good many more years.

He had often put foxes and stray dogs to flight and it was mainly for that reason that the old widow maintained him as a protector of her chickens and ducks. Not having a flock of geese for company seemed to make him extra vicious.

He spent his time patrolling up and down the nearby River Moy, chasing young anglers away from his domain. Some of those anglers swore his skull must have been armour-plated as they hopped heaps of stones off it to no avail.

One day, when a teaman, as tea sellers were known back then, called to the widow to sell her a pound or two of tea, the gander strode up to his pony and bit him on the heel, causing him to run away. The wagon was turned over and the stock of tea was spilt all over the road.

The teaman threatened legal proceedings against the widow, who decided it was time to eliminate the gander. On the very next night, two IRA men on the run called to the widow's house for a cup of tea.

She asked them to kill a goose for her and invited them to return the next day to share the dinner with her. Being natives of a neighbouring town, they hadn't the slightest idea of how to go about killing a goose.

Finally, after a hard struggle, they managed to catch the gander; one executioner grabbed his body and stretched his long neck over a wooden block the widow used for chopping firewood. His companion grabbed the widow's firewood axe and, with a mighty blow, he severed the gander's head from his body. Both men jumped back to avoid bloodstains. Without warning, the headless bird rose into the air and made a long, slanting dive towards the Moy, which was in flood at the time.

There was a swift current at that point and the headless corpse was swept rapidly downstream. The two men sympathised with the widow and promised to make up her loss in some way.

They got a young schoolboy to carry a message through to some sympathisers in Swinford and ordered 2lb of bacon rashers and 2lb of sausages.

Pork sausages were new to the market back then and the casing or skins of those new arrivals were many times thicker than those of their modern-day counterparts. After procuring the bacon and sausages, the two men returned to the widow and delivered the parcel. She thanked them and invited them to return that night to share a meal with her when she had the bacon and sausages fried.

They duly came back a couple of hours later to find a plate of rashers served up with a pile of what resembled charred, shrivelled skins. When one of the men asked her what had happened to the sausages, she replied, 'Sausages? Is that what they are called? Well, when I got the dirty things cleaned out and rinsed, they were hardly worth cooking!'

38

BRICK MAKING

S eeing a kiln of bricks being 'burned' after going through all the preparatory rituals in brick production is one of my earliest recollections. My father, grandfather and great-grandfather managed a small, handmade brick industry in Ballydrum, Swinford, from around 1825 until 1920. This was a seasonal operation, confined to the summer months as sun-drying the freshly made bricks was one of the imperative initial steps in brick production.

The deposits of brick clay which existed in this neighbourhood were blue boulder clay, carried down by the River Moy and deposited in lowland flats by backwash action. Those deposits usually varied from 2 to 8 feet.

This clay went under several names, including 'dobe' and 'daab', which was the most popular term. The clay being prepared for brick production was first lifted manually above ground. It had to be mixed, sliced and turned over several times and pressed down with heavy planks to get a pliable, even mixture, free of air pockets. There were no excavators or manual diggers in those days.

Incidentally, the first steam-driven excavator seen in Mayo was employed in the construction of the Claremorris–Ballinrobe railway almost a century ago. It was instrumental in cutting the Hill of Caltra to a depth of 95 feet. It was nicknamed 'The American Devil' and people travelled long distances to see this wonder.

When ready for moulding, as the shaping process was called, the clay had the texture and consistency of soft putty. The spread ground had to be level and sanded over to prevent the freshly made bricks from sticking to the ground. The moulder took his stand with his pile of moulds at the moulder's table. He had to pack the clay firmly into the wooden shapes, which usually measured 9 by 4 by 2½ inches. He levelled off the clay in the mould with a deft sweep of a rounded stick.

Three spreaders, working at top speed, took the filled moulds away and emptied the raw bricks onto the smooth and sanded ground, returning with the moulds for a refill. Two good moulders working very long hours could turn out 4,500 bricks per day.

Around 1890, the pay of a moulder was three shillings a day and that of other labourers was two shillings. The extra shilling for moulders was envied and viewed as a big differential in those days.

After some time on the spread ground, the bricks, if sufficiently sun-dried, were turned over like sods of peat and later stacked in square piles close to the kiln.

Inside the kiln, six fire tunnels or arches measuring 3 feet high by 2 feet wide were constructed at ground level and extended the full length of the kiln. These arches were filled with turf and set alight; a continuous fire had to be maintained until the bricks were sufficiently burned or baked. This could be four and a half to five and a half days, according to wind and weather conditions, the quality of the turf and other factors.

It was an unwritten law that two men had to attend the burning kiln at night. An old man told me that he enjoyed being one of the night-watchers while the kiln was burning. He said that one of their favourite pastimes was cooking a fat chicken or succulent young duck in one of the fire arches of the kiln.

After the fowl was killed, they merely covered it with soft 'daab' and placed it in one of the arches close to the entrance. After the bird was cooked, all the feathers were reduced to a black smear and the intestines were shrivelled up by the intense heat. As for the flesh, he said, 'You'd be licking your lips after you ate it.'

In those days, over 100 years ago, wealthy shopkeepers' sons and other young 'gods' from the Swinford area formed a club called the Cock and Hen Club or, alternatively, the Duck and Hen Club. It was so called because of the practice of going out into the countryside and raiding fowl houses for birds to capture and cook after taking them back to town. The feast usually ended with a good soak of spirits.

'One night,' said my informant, 'we heard the fowl in a house a short distance away making a loud racket. It was a very bright night and as we rushed to the fowl house we surprised three intruders who took to their heels. They seemed to be half drunk and the two dogs we had with us gave them such a mauling that they were not seen around again.'

Around 1895, a journeyman potter from North Leitrim or Fermanagh, whose name, as far as I can recollect, was Jim Mullen, came to Ballydrum. He had his own potter's wheel and after a deal was struck with my father, he started to make butter and milk crocks, flower pots and other types of household receptacles.

He built a small kiln like a beehive to bake his wares. He had a pony and a small spring cart and he visited all the small towns within a 25-mile radius to sell his products in their marketplaces.

After two or three seasons, he left to start operations in his native place. He was known locally as 'Jim the Crocks'. Glazing his crocks was a secret he guarded jealously at all times.

Brick-making operations employed a staff of between sixteen and twenty-four, according to business fluctuations. This included two or three carters for delivering bricks. About 500 cart loads of turf were burned annually in brickmaking in Ballydrum. The most popular size kiln of bricks contained 50,000 of them. When 'well burned', to use a local term, the bricks turned from blue to red owing to the transformation of the iron oxide in the brick clay.

Cement was slowly gaining in popularity at the beginning of the twentieth century and sounded the death knell for all the small brick works in the country. They had mostly disappeared by the start of the First World War as concrete was faster to prepare and utilise and was also a less labourious substance for building purposes.

39

IN CAPTAIN HOUSTON'S COUNTRY

When Captain Boswell Houston died at his Doo Lough Lodge in the south-west Mayo highlands in 1872, like so many more that came to conquer and colonise, he departed this life saddened, embittered and frustrated.

Having served the British Empire well with the 10th Hussars in the conquering and colonising of large tracts of Africa, he decided to retire to the largely unspoilt and untamed West of Ireland to give the natives the benefit of his ideas and experience. Having received huge tracts of land from the Crown and from Lord Sligo inside of three years, he was said to own 12,000 head of sheep and also a large number of horses and cattle. The area stretched from Killary Bay to within a stone's throw of Croaghpatrick, embracing the Muilrea, Sheeffry and Ben Gorm range of mountains.

Commencing on a peaceful note, he soon changed his attitude as he found that his ever-increasing herds of livestock required more land – if the rough, heathery slopes from Bundorragha to Loughta could be called land. He established a policy of tenant evictions, which his wife described as 'a true form of mercy to the poor, poverty-stricken natives'. 'The Scotchman', as Houston is known down to the present day, soon found to his cost that the poverty-stricken natives were not as easily cowed as the 'little brown natives of Africa'.

An old man from Derrygarbh told me that his great-grandfather saw 500 'smokes' in Tullaghbawn before the famine and before the

Scotchman and his evictions came to lay waste the countryside. In the warm summer of 1856, many of the Scotchman's evicted tenants did not leave the county as he had hoped. Instead, they squatted in remote mountain retreats and lived on the fattest of Houston's sheep. With four or five shepherds and half a dozen sheepdogs, he tried to keep constant vigil over his countless thousands of sheep. However, a ringleader of the evicted tenants solved the problem of the tracker dogs.

He met a Galway man with his own ideas of landlords and land grabbers at the Pattern of Leenane. The Galway man gave him a recipe to poison the Scotchman's dogs and one morning Houston woke to find six or seven dead dogs outside his front door. To the Scotchman, this was a challenge for all-out war. He came down heavily on trout and salmon poachers as he lived in one of the best fishing areas of the world. One local poacher, named the *Rí Eascóin* (King Eel), retaliated by 'milking' salmon outside Houston's front door. This consisted of squeezing the milt from the spawn-sick salmon.

Then the Scotchman played his last card. He compelled three or four of his herders to live on mountain peaks in rough huts so they could keep a watch on the sheep and a lookout for the sheep rustlers. The rustlers got a few active lads to dress in sheepskins, infiltrate the

flock at nightfall, and grab and make off with their prey as night settled down.

After his death, Houston's widow wrote her book, *True Story of a
Modern Exile*, telling his experiences in County Mayo. In her book,
Mrs Houston complained of the almost constant storms and frequent torrential downpours of Delphi, Doolough and Glenamurra.
This region has been recorded in different years as having the highest annual rainfall in Western Europe. Therefore, her complaint was
not without foundation.

40

BRIAN RUA AND THE ACHILL RAILWAY

I t may well have been mere coincidence that the first and the last trains to run on the Westport to Achill line carried coffins of persons who had met unexpected deaths. However, those people who have heard of the 'Prophet of Erris' might not agree.

Brian Rua Ó Cearbháin (Red-haired Brian Carbine) was born in 1648. He was a small farmer, like most of his neighbours. He was unremarkable in all respects until it was discovered that he had developed the gift of prophecy in middle age.

According to local lore, as he passed along the road one day, he chanced to overhear a poor widow asking her landlord for more time to pay her rent. The landlord wanted to know if there was anyone who would go surety for her.

The old woman replied that she had no one to act as guarantor for her except God, in whom she placed her trust, to which the landlord responded, 'I'd much prefer it if you had anybody but God to back you up.'

Brian Rua took pity on the woman and paid her rent for her. He said he would put his trust in God to repay him his money. On his way home, he was feeling tired so he sat down at the roadside to have a rest. He fell asleep and when he awoke, he discovered a jewel in the right sleeve of his coat. It turned out that by caressing this jewel, he was able to foresee events that had yet to happen.

In 1678 the local parish priest, Father Higgins, instructed his parishioners not to associate with Ó Cearbháin as he was in the pay of the devil. Brian Rua retorted by saying that the priest would become a Protestant minister in four weeks!

Incredibly, this prediction came to pass.

It seems he was able to read and write, in contrast to the people around him, and he wrote down prophecies of events that he sensed would happen sometime in the future. Unfortunately for posterity, his son grabbed his documents during one of their frequent fights and threw them into the fire.

In 1906 a noted Celtic scholar, Michael Timoney, collected all the stories he could find about Ó Cearbháin and his visions from the older people in the Erris region. The stories had been handed down from one generation to the succeeding one by word of mouth. The collection was called '*Tarngaireacht Bhrian Ruadh*' (Brian Rua's Prophecies). It was subsequently translated into English.

Was Brian Rua really a seer who could foretell the future or were his so-called predictions just figments of gullible people's imaginations? The fact is that most of his 'visions' can be treated with scepticism, but there are exceptions – including the one that foresaw the arrival of the railway line between Westport and Achill.

This is a translation of what Timoney recorded: 'Carriages on wheels with smoke and fire will come to Achill and the first and last carriages will carry dead bodies.'

This prediction was unfortunately borne out, for the first passenger train service from Westport to Achill in 1884 carried the coffins of thirty-two young people who drowned when the boat they were on capsized in Clew Bay, near Westport Harbour. They were on a boat going to meet a steamer that would have taken them to Scotland for seasonal work picking potatoes.

The second part of Ó Cearbháin's grim prediction was fulfilled in 1937 when the bodies of ten youngsters were carried on the last train to Achill. The boys were 'Tatie Hokers', seasonal workers from Achill and other impoverished parts of the country who went to Scotland to pick potatoes. They worked for a pittance and were treated with contempt by their employers. These children had been sleeping in a disused bothy or cow shed in the town of Kirkintollach when the building caught fire and they were unable to escape.

This was the last train journey from Westport to Achill and the service was thereafter discontinued. Timoney recorded this prophecy in 1906, over thirty years *before* the last train to Achill carried their coffins home.

Like Nostradamus, Ó Cearbháin couched his predictions in cryptic, unclear language that in some cases could have a number of different meanings, but some are quite unambiguous.

To somebody who has heard of the Great Famine of the 1840s, when potato crops rotted in the fields, the reference to roads of meal is clear; roads were built as part of a government-backed initiative to alleviate the food shortage whereby the workers got allowances of cornmeal instead of wages.

Some of his other prophecies were:

- Paupers will be wearing shoes and children will speak English.
- There will be a year of plenty, followed by a year of grief and another few years and not many will survive.
- News will travel on the top of poles faster than a hawk will fly from Dublin to Blacksod Bay.

- There will be a road across every bog and the roads will have ribbons of eyes.
- A bridge will be made over the Abhainn Mór River at Bellacorick and it will never be finished.
- People will be imprisoned without crime or cause, and it is a wise man that leaves the country.
- Carriages travelling north and south will have iron wheels and the stones on the roads will be talking.
- Roads of meal will be made all over Ireland and a half-penny candle will burn all the money in the country.

The last prophecy is particularly interesting as it refers to an event that took place in the 1840s, more than a century after Ó Cearbháin's death: the Great Famine of the 1840s, when the potato crops during the latter years of that decade were devastated by blight. (This was catastrophic for the poorer classes for whom the potato was the staple diet. A series of relief works were carried out where the workers were paid in corn meal.) The second part of this prophecy remains unclear.

Those who deride his 'prophecies' may have plenty of rational reasons to do so but there are compelling facts that need to be borne in mind if you follow the sceptic's route.

One of them has already been mentioned – the last train to Achill carried dead bodies – but the other, although less obvious, is equally pertinent. If that prophecy is a fake, it must have been added sometime after the potato crops began to rot in the fields and famine relief work was undertaken. The accounts of Brian's life and his predictions were handed down through the generations after his death by means of the oral tradition. However, if the 'roads of meal' prophecy had been added after the crops began to rot then the people who passed on such accounts to Timoney would not have accepted it as genuine.

As people huddled around some fireside or other in their localities to while away the long hours of darkness on winter evenings, they passed the time telling and listening to stories. Stories about Brian Rua, as with all tales worthy of being handed down through generations, were passed on without change of any sort. That's because the listeners at such storytelling sessions would have heard each account over and over again. If there was even one word altered from one session to the next, there would have been howls of protest. So, it is extremely unlikely that prophecies as we hear or read them today would not be the very same as those composed by Brian Rua's contemporaries, none of whom ever heard of Balfour Lines or have an idea of what they were.

The Balfour Lines that appear to have fulfilled Brian Rua's predictions of the Achill railway were the brainchild of Arthur Balfour, who was appointed Chief Secretary for Ireland in the 1887. Balfour was an energetic and compassionate individual who sought to lift the morale and economic status of the poorer people in Irish society. Around the time of his appointment, Irish politics were in a state of turmoil. Agrarian unrest was widespread as tenant farmers and their supporters clamoured for the introduction of the '3Fs'; Free Sale (of their holdings), Fair Rent, and Fixity of Tenure, which meant that a tenant could not be evicted as long as the rents were paid on time. The Nationalists (the leading constitutionalist political party) sought Home Rule – a limited form of self-government – and were increasing their support all the time.

Balfour engaged in a policy of 'Killing Home Rule with Kindness'. Basically, this meant providing employment in areas hard hit by poverty to encourage disaffected elements to tone down their demands for political change.

Among a series of measures to bring this about, he had three railway lines built in extremely disadvantaged areas where commercial railway companies would not go. One of them was the line from Westport along the Atlantic coast to Achill, 44km due north.

The first station on this extension was Newport, which opened in February 1894, followed by Mallaranny, (Mulranny) in August of the same year. The line to Achill was completed in May 1895.

After the railway line was shut down due to a fall in business, the tracks were lifted and the lands through which it passed reverted to their original owners. It remained thus for more than fifty years until somebody thought of re-opening the route again as a greenway, an off-road path for cyclists and pedestrians, which is today a spectacular traffic-free trail to escape the hustle and bustle of modern life.

A relatively simple idea has proved to be very popular with people from all walks of life and of all ages. Tourism sources in Achill have said that an average of 300 greenway users visit Achill daily.

Those travelling the greenway are surrounded by open country-side for most of the journey. The views along the route are stunning, with the spectacular Nephin Beg mountain range on one side and Croagh Patrick on the far side of Clew Bay and its countless islets on the other. Users of this facility can break the full length of the trail into three sections, corresponding to the intermediate stops along the original line.

Cyclists who are unable to bring their own bikes along can rent them in any town along the route and can also leave them at the most convenient one. Hire companies provide a shuttle bus service to return them to their starting point.

What the future holds for the greenway and those who live in the vicinity is unclear, but it's the nature of such places to undergo change and who knows what the next development may be? To make matters worse, we can't turn to Brian Rua's prophecies for guidance because he had nothing to say about the railway after predicting its last sad journey.

41

THE DOOLOUGH
TRAGEDY

A simple Celtic stone stands at the roadside a short distance north of Doolough, beside the road from Leenaune to Louisburgh. Driving along this usually deserted stretch of road, one could easily pass it by without paying much notice to it or wondering what the reason for its presence at that spot may have been.

It is a famine memorial, a reminder of the Great Famine, the shortage of potatoes which occurred in Ireland during the mid-nineteenth century, and commemorates one of the most tragic events during that terrible period in Irish history. The memorial itself is a plain stone cross engraved with the words 'Doolough Tragedy 1849'.

As a classic example of man's inhumanity to man (and woman and child also), the Doolough Tragedy cannot be surpassed.

On 29 March, a multitude of starving people assembled at Louisburgh workhouse, desperately awaiting the arrival of two officials from Westport Poor Law Union.

The Receiving Officer at Louisburgh workhouse had told them that he did not have the authority to issue them with food or with a ticket that would admit them to the workhouse, but he further informed them that two officials were on their way from Westport and that they would have the authority to decide what should be done in each individual case. After a fruitless wait of several hours in the icy wind, the pitiable wretches were told that the two gentlemen had gone to Delphi Lodge, a hunting lodge about 12 miles south of Louisburgh, to spend the night there. (The lodge was built in the 1830s by the Marquis of Sligo for hunting and fishing. It was named after the valley's alleged similarity to the home of the Oracle in Greece.)

The people who had gathered outside of the workhouse were then instructed to appear at Delphi Lodge at seven o'clock the following morning if they wished to continue receiving relief. So, the starving multitude had to undertake an extremely fatiguing journey in very bad weather.

Worse was to follow, for when they finally arrived at the lodge, they found that the two officers refused to meet them. The worthy gentlemen were having dinner and were not to be disturbed.

Finally, when they had finished their meal, they refused to give either an entrance ticket to the workhouse or food relief (3lb of Indian meal) to anyone outside in the freezing conditions.

During the walk back to Louisburgh, many perished along the shores of Doolough. A letter written to the Mayo Constitution at the time indicated that sixteen people died along the trail. However, according to local tradition, up to 400 people may have perished between Louisburgh and Delphi – many of them so frail and weak that they were blown into the lake by the strong wind. Corpses were found by the roadside, some of them with grass in their mouths from one last futile attempt at nourishment.

The next day, the Receiving Officer at the Louisburgh workhouse sent a group of men out along the road to collect and bury the bodies where they had fallen. One contemporary account stated that the road was covered with corpses 'as numerous as sheaves of corn in an autumn field'.

An annual walk is held along this route in memory of the Doolough dead and to highlight the starvation of the world's poor today.

42

CHARLES BOYCOTT

'Captain' Charles Cunningham Boycott was a farmer who moved to the Ballinrobe area from Achill Island in 1873. He moved into Lough Mask House, owned by Lord Erne, 6km from Ballinrobe. Initially he leased a farm of 300 acres from Erne and in May 1874 he took a lease on Lough Mask House and farm for thirty-one years at £402 per annum for the first nine years, and £500 per annum for the remaining twenty-two years. In doing so, he unknowingly began his march into history.

Although he was a tenant farmer as well as being the agent for a landlord, he was probably the biggest employer in the area and got on well with the local tradespeople: labourers, grooms, coachmen and house servants who found employment with him.

When he initially moved to the area, he had been on good terms with the local community, but a rift developed between Boycott and his tenants as time went on. He had become a magistrate and was also an Englishman, which may have contributed to his unpopularity.

Boycott may have felt that he was a popular figure in the locality, but his tenants soon began to complain. They said that he had laid down many restrictions, such as not allowing gates to be left open and not allowing hens to trespass on his property, and he fined anyone who transgressed these petty restrictions. He had also withdrawn privileges from the tenants, such as the right to collect wood from the estate. In August 1880, his labourers went on strike in a dispute over wages.

Lord Erne preferred Englishmen or Scots in positions of authority, and the title of 'Captain', most likely bestowed on Boycott by his neighbours for obvious reasons, may have played a part in getting him the appointment. To the surprise of those who thought they were making fun of his airs and graces, he quite liked the title, as he felt it elevated his standing amongst the gentry in the region.

He had, in fact, had a career in the British army, but it was an undistinguished one. In 1848 he entered the Royal Military Academy at Woolwich, hoping to serve in the Corps of Royal Sappers and Miners. However, he was discharged the following year after failing an exam. In 1850 his family bought him a commission in the 39th Foot Regiment for £450.

He served some time in this regiment, from which was transferred to Ireland. He served three years in the army, but then he resigned and sold his commission. He decided to remain in Ireland, where he leased a farm in Tipperary before moving to Achill Island.

By all accounts, he was a progressive and capable farmer and since Lord Erne's land was situated in the fertile limestone region of South Mayo, there was no apparent reason why his arrival should not have been welcomed by the local community. He had, he thought, found the home where he would spend the remainder of his days, but it was to prove to be the wrong place and the wrong time. The land at Lough Mask was much better than his holding on Achill and Boycott's experience on the island stood to him; he farmed well and prospered. He kept a few racehorses, which he often rode at local meetings with some success, and he hunted, shot and fished in season.

In this period of Irish history, landlords, many of them absentee, owned 80 per cent of all the land of Ireland, while 50 per cent of tenants occupied holdings of less than 15 acres; more than three quarters of all holdings were annual tenancies. Boycott was in a position of power and he knew it.

As Erne's agent, he had a duty to collect the rents from the thirty-five tenants and generally look after the estate. At this stage, after twenty years in the county, he considered himself a Mayo man.

In the late 1870s, a widespread economic downturn had caused a crisis in Irish agriculture; rack-renting and mass evictions were the order of the day, and famine was a constant threat in the west. There was a worldwide economic depression that lasted from 1873 until 1879 and prices were artificially reduced.

James Daly, a native of Lahardane, County Mayo, and editor and joint owner of the *Connaught Telegraph* newspaper, organised a mass meeting of tenants at Irishtown on 20 April 1879 to protest against their landlord, Canon Geoffrey Bourke, and forced him to withdraw eviction notices and reduce the rents of his tenants by 25 per cent. Over 8,000 people turned up for the meeting, which was truly remarkable as most who attended had to walk there. The show of widespread solidarity intimidated the canon and others of his class into avoiding confrontation and they therefore met the rent reduction demands.

Arising from the success of this meeting, the Irish National Land League was founded at the Imperial Hotel in Castlebar on 21 October 1879. At that meeting Charles Stewart Parnell was elected president of the League and Michael Davitt was appointed one of the honorary secretaries.

Strange as it may seem, Canon Bourke appeared at a League protest meeting some months later and sat on the platform. It seems he felt he was legally unable to lower the rents that led to the Irishtown meeting because he was holding the land in trust for his two nephews at that time. His brother was serving in the army in India and asked the canon to oversee his property in his absence. Once founded, the League began to look for an opportunity to keep the protest momentum going.

The leader of the new protest movement, Charles Stewart Parnell, made his feelings known when he advised the common people to remove co-operation of any sort with landlords and agents who were not prepared to allow any rent reduction in those hard economic times.

Boycott presented him with an ideal target.

'Shun him in the streets of the town, you must shun him in the shop, you must shun him in the fairgreen and in the marketplace, and even in the place of worship, by leaving him alone, by putting him in a moral Coventry, by isolating him from the rest of his country as if he were the leper of old, you must show your detestation of the crime he has committed.'

This new form of protest was effective on Erne's estate; there was a withdrawal of the local labour required to harvest the crops, the refusal of shops in nearby Ballinrobe to serve him, and the withdrawal of laundry services and the delivery of mail. According to Boycott, an 12-year-old boy who attempted to collect his mail was threatened with violence if he continued.

Boycott, with instructions from Lord Erne, was prepared to allow a 10 per cent reduction in the rents. Most of the tenants insisted on a 25 per cent reduction.

He decided to serve eviction notices on eleven of his tenants, with momentous consequences.

On 22 September, five months after the Irishtown meeting, David Sears, a process-server, with an escort of seventeen RIC constables, began serving Lord Erne's defaulting tenants around the Neale with eviction notices. However, he and his escort were soon forced back to Lough Mask House by a group of local women, throwing stones, mud, manure and anything else that came to hand at them. The following day, the farm was invaded by a mob of up to 100 people and his workforce warned off.

Local curate Fr O'Malley is reported as having congratulated them on 'the great victory you have achieved and the noble example you have set'. There is a local legend that O'Malley had a falling-out with Boycott around that time; he had sent one of Boycott's workers, a man named Branigan, to ask the 'Captain' for a site for a Catholic school and Boycott, not unreasonably, had inquired why he had not come himself. (O'Malley is also credited with coining the verb 'boycott', saying that the people would not be able to remember 'ostracise'.)

Boycott now found himself in a difficult situation, as he had horses, cattle, sheep and poultry to look after and crops to get in with very few helpers. Three of his staff refused to leave (Johnny Meany, a groom and former jockey, Judy, the cook, and Harriet, a parlour maid) and he had four guests staying at the time, a teenage niece and her fiancé, and two teenage nephews. They carried on as best they could, rising at 4 a.m., with the men being escorted everywhere by armed police, but at night fences and gates were broken, trees and hedges felled and crops stolen or ruined. Boycott was in a fix but was determined to do his duty and see it through. He said at the time, 'I can hardly desert Lord Erne and moreover my own property is sunk in this place.'

The people who refused to deal with him on any account no doubt suffered financially, but they received partial relief from Land League funds and between this help and threats of intimidation from their neighbours, they were determined to hold out until their demands were met. Boycott thought he could break the resolve of his former suppliers in Ballinrobe by offering ready cash for their products, but in this he was unsuccessful. One day a person acting on his behalf entered a small drapery shop in the town, accompanied by an RIC officer. He pointed at a shirt in the window and offered to buy it on the spot.

But the old woman who owned the business waved his money away, saying that the garment in question had been sold to a man from Partry and she was awaiting his arrival to collect it. Undaunted, Boycott's agent said he'd buy another one but the old lady told him that she couldn't sell him that one either. As a matter of fact, she said that she could not sell him a single item in the shop as everything had already been sold and was awaiting collection. Boycott had to accept that without outside help he had little hope of success against the Land League and the indomitable Fr O'Malley.

Tensions were rising in rural Mayo, as elsewhere, and the term 'agrarian unrest' had become commonplace. Indeed, the term was to be heard on all sides as tenants and supporters resorted to violence to further their demands.

William Sydney Clements, the 3rd Earl of Leitrim, had been murdered on 2 April 1878 at Cratlagh Wood, near Milford in County Donegal, after he had threatened to evict twenty of his tenants. On 25 September 1880, Lord Mountmorres was assassinated near his home at Clonbur, County Galway. On 14 October 1880, Boycott wrote to the *London Times* setting out his predicament and this led to the dispute, which until then had been a relatively minor affair little known outside of Mayo, gaining international notice:

THE STATE OF IRELAND

Sir, The following detail may be interesting to your readers as exemplifying the power of the Land League. On 22 September a process-server, escorted by a police force of seventeen men, retreated to my house for protection, followed by a howling mob of people, who yelled and hooted at the members of my family. On the ensuing day, 23 September, the people collected in crowds upon my farm, and some hundred or so came up to my house and ordered off, under threats of ulterior consequences, all my farm labourers, workmen, and stablemen, commanding them never to work for me again. My herd has been frightened by them into giving up his employment, though he has refused to give up the house he held from me as part of his emolument. Another herd on an off farm has also been compelled to resign his situation. My blacksmith has received a letter threatening him with murder if he does any more work for me, and my laundress has also been ordered to give up my washing. A little boy, twelve years of age, who carried my post-bag to and from the neighbouring town of Ballinrobe, was struck and threatened on 27 September, and ordered to desist from his work; since which time I have sent my little nephew for my letters and even he, on 2nd October, was stopped on the road and threatened if he continued to act as my messenger. The shopkeepers have been warned to stop all supplies to my house, and I have just received a message from the post mistress to say that the telegraph messenger was stopped and threatened on the road when bringing out a message to me and that she does not think it safe to send any telegrams which may come for me in the future for fear they should be abstracted and the messenger injured. My farm is public property; the people wander over it with impunity. My crops are trampled upon, carried away in quantities, and destroyed wholesale. The locks on my gates are smashed, the gates thrown open, the walls thrown down, and the stock driven out on the roads. I can get no workmen to do anything, and my ruin is openly avowed as the object of the Land League unless I throw up everything and leave the country. I say nothing about the danger to my own life, which is apparent to anybody who knows the country.

CHARLES C. BOYCOTT

Lough Mask House, County Mayo, 14 October.

On 29 October the *Dublin Daily Express* proposed the setting-up of a fund to save Boycott's crops. This was adopted enthusiastically in Ulster, where Lord Erne lived at Crom Castle in County Fermanagh, and plans were laid for the 'Boycott Relief Expedition'.

Boycott needed and sought no more than twelve men to harvest his 8 acres of turnips, 7 acres of mangolds, 2 acres of potatoes and to thresh 20 acres of already-cut corn, but by the first week in November 1880 the matter was out of his hands; the Ulster 'Boycott Relief Expedition' had organised fifty volunteers, Orangemen from Cavan and Monaghan, to harvest the Captain's crops.

The volunteers arrived at Lough Mask House on 12 November, escorted by a large company of soldiers, having had to walk all the way from Claremorris railway station in the driving rain as none of the local drivers would carry them. They were accommodated in tents on the lawns, in barns and in the boathouse.

Around 900 soldiers were stationed in and around Ballinrobe and the Neale for the next two weeks until the harvesting was finished. A large number of sheep, fowl and other foodstuffs vanished while they were there; they also turned Boycott's well-tended paths and lawns into an appalling quagmire. On 27 November they left, along with the relief expedition, and it was reckoned that it had cost up to £10,000 to save a harvest worth at most £350.

The *Connaught Telegraph* gave extensive coverage to the episode and, under the heading 'OUR INVADERS', James Daly recorded the miserable state of the rain-sodden volunteers and soldiers and, as was his wont, called for restraint by hotheads to avoid any danger of bloodshed.

Left without protection, and with no alternative, the following day Captain Boycott and his wife Annie sadly left their home in an army ambulance wagon, escorted by a troop of the 19th Hussars. In Dublin they were escorted from the train to the Hammam Hotel, where they got a mixed reception from the general public, many of whom had Nationalist sympathies. On 1 December 1880, they took the mail boat to Holyhead.

The affair made headlines worldwide. Boycott was now a legendary and a notorious figure. By the end of 1880, 'boycotting' was widespread in Ireland and further afield and within twenty years the word would appear in dictionaries all over the world. In spring 1881, travelling as Mr and Mrs Charles Cunningham, the Boycotts sailed for the US to visit their friends. It had been a long, hard winter for Boycott and he recovered his health and his humour on his first visit to the New World.

In August 1881, the Boycotts returned quietly to Ireland and to Lough Mask House and found that nothing had been lost or stolen in their absence. It is probable that when they were forced to leave, an Ulsterman was installed as caretaker, as had been the case in other similar situations. Mayo lore has it that they were warmly welcomed home by the local people, as if nothing had happened.

In December 1880, Boycott had written to Prime Minister Gladstone seeking £6,000 compensation for the losses that he sustained 'due to the absence of law in the West of Ireland'. He was unsuccessful and finally had to face the fact that he could no longer afford to stay on at Lough Mask House.

The day Charles Cunningham Boycott died, aged 65 and a technical bankrupt, nearly the whole of the Royal Navy was lined up in the Solent and beyond, with its admirals and its bands; sirens sounded, flags and pennants fluttered in the warm breeze, and church bells pealed out loudly across the length and breadth of the UK.

But this frenetic activity had nothing to do with Boycott's passing. It was 19 June 1897 and Queen Victoria was celebrating her Diamond Jubilee. His burial service in Burgh St Peter church was conducted by the Revd Douglas Boycott, one of the nephews who had been with him during the famous 'siege' seventeen years earlier at Lough Mask House.

43

THE LOUGH MASK MURDERS

It is hard to believe while driving through the barren country-side between Lough Nafooey and Lough Mask that people ever lived there. But they did, in their hundreds, during the nineteenth century and well into the following one. The numbers, though greatly depleted by the Great Famine, were still high four decades after that dreadful event. Landlords still demanded their rents and had those who failed to pay evicted from their miserable cabins, but there was a growing air of defiance among the peasantry, many of whom had survived the terrible famine and were not prepared to relive that experience again if they could help it.

In the late 1870s there were fears that another famine was immi-nent. Widespread evictions were taking place as a combination of bad weather and falling agricultural prices left many tenants unable to pay their rents. Agrarian violence broke out on a wide scale; land-lords and their bailiffs were targeted and many were assassinated; the security forces tried hard to secure convictions but in tightly knit communities, few would dare to give evidence.

Bribery was used to induce some less than credible witnesses to stand up in court and send their neighbours to the gallows. Looking back, it is obvious that the authorities weren't too fussy about whether those brought to court were actually guilty or not. It seems that securing a conviction took precedence over any other consideration.

The accused in such cases were almost invariably Irish speakers who knew next to nothing about the intricacies of the legal system.

On the other hand, juries, lawyers and judges spoke only English and in many cases an interpreter wasn't employed to act as a go-between. Securing convictions meant favourable publicity in the international press, as events in Ireland at this time were making headlines worldwide.

Such was the case in South Mayo in 1882 when two high-profile, multiple killings took place in the vicinity of Lough Mask.

One became known far and wide as 'The Lough Mask Murders', when two bailiffs working for Lord Ardilaun were killed. According to local media, they were 'an old man and a lad'.

Tensions had arisen in the area during the Land War, which had begun some years earlier. The old man, Joseph Huddy, was a bailiff on Lord Ardilaun's estate and part of his duty was to serve notice of eviction on tenants who had fallen behind with their rent payments. The lad was his grandson, John Huddy.

According to George Bolton, the state solicitor who presented the prosecution's case when suspects were arrested and were sent forward for trial, Joseph Huddy, the bailiff, set out on 3 January 1882 to deliver a number of notices. He brought his teenage grandson along as he moved from village to village. At some stage of their journey, they were confronted and shot and their bodies were stuffed into sacks and thrown into the waters of Lough Mask. Nobody knew why Joseph Huddy set about his mission without bringing armed guards with him for protection. There had been numerous instances of attacks on landlords and their agents throughout the country which resulted in a number of fatalities. In 1880, Lord Montmorres, who was portrayed in some newspapers as a kindly landlord, was killed by a flurry of shots as he was driving himself home after a magistrates' meeting in Clonbur. This happened in the vicinity of Clonbur, a little village not far from the spot where the Huddys were killed.

Yet the agent and his grandson set out upon their nefarious work in a casual manner, as if they expected to be made welcome wherever they went.

When they failed to return home, a murder inquiry began. The security forces went to extraordinary lengths to find their bodies, and, as part of the exertions, a steam launch, the *Valorous*, was brought across the country from one of Her Majesty's ships in Killery Harbour to dredge the lough. On 26 January, twenty-three days after their disappearance, both bodies were raised from the lough.

Lough Mask is the greatest lake by volume of water in the Irish republic, with depths of up to 60 metres in places, so the assassins, who knew the lough, must have felt the bodies would never be found. Both Huddys were found to have been killed by pistol shots. Each of them was found tied up in a sack, with weights attached to keep them from rising.

A search for the murderers began. Four men were eventually arrested and put on trial in Dublin in December of the same year. Three of them were found guilty and were hanged: they were Patrick Higgins, Thomas Higgins and Michael Flynn. The fourth defendant, also named Patrick Higgins, was spared because the Crown accepted that he had been compelled to take part in the murders.

Some witnesses had eventually came forward to testify and to name the parties being tried for murder, but nobody, except the judge, appeared to place any credence in what they had to say. However, a confused elderly woman, Margaret O'Donnell, did admit in the end that she had seen several men throwing sacks into the lake and pointed out the spot where this took place. Her evidence made the task of finding the bodies much easier, but had fatal consequences for herself and her family, who lived on nearby Maamtrasna Mountain.

The old lady had been staying with her son, whose cottage overlooked the lake, but she lived with her son-in-law, John Joyce, in the remote hamlet of Cappanacreha. On the morning of 17 August of the same year, a neighbour called to the Joyce house on an errand.

He found the door pulled away and John Joyce lying dead on the floor, naked. Returning to the house with other villagers, they quickly discovered three more bodies – Joyce's aged mother-in-law, Margaret, his wife Bridget, whose skull had been crushed, and the corpse of his daughter, Peggy. Two boys were seriously wounded – Michael, aged 17, had been shot in the stomach and head and later died. Patsy, aged 10, survived.

This massacre occurred against a backdrop of widespread violence. The Land League had been established in Castlebar in 1879 by Michael Davitt, a former Fenian prisoner. A massive protest meeting had taken place in Irishtown, a hamlet 5km east of Ballindine on the N17. Over 8,000 people attended this rally held in protest against the rent increases being sought by a local landlord. The meeting was a success, with the landlord agreeing not to raise the rent of his tenants.

The League challenged the rights of landlords to raise rents at will and to evict tenants without the right of appeal. Secret societies had been founded with the aim of fighting back against the cruelties of landlords and their acts of violence, which had became commonplace. The agent of the hated Lord Clanricarde was shot dead and the killings had become indiscriminate. Tensions were heightening and it was inevitable that blood was going to be shed.

However, the massacre of the Joyces stood out because of the ferocity of the attack. The case attracted widespread media attention. Two days after the murders, *The Times* reported that:

> No ingenuity can exaggerate the brutal ferocity of a crime which spared neither the grey hairs of an aged woman nor the innocent child of 12 years who slept beside her. It is an outburst of unredeemed and inexplicable savagery before which one stands appalled, and oppressed with a painful sense of the failure of our vaunted civilisation.

Ten men were arrested and put on trial for their lives. However, what passed for a trial was in fact a travesty of justice. The proceedings were conducted in English while the accused were Irish speakers and couldn't understand what was going on. The prosecution case was a farrago of deceits and the defence was lamentable – simply going through the motions. The defence lawyer was a 24-year-old Trinity College student who didn't speak or understand Irish.

Myles Joyce, one of the three men who was subsequently executed, never had a chance, even though one of the men hanged at the same time as him signed a declaration saying he had no part in the murders.

His heavily pregnant wife, Brighid, wrote a pitiful appeal to the editor of the *Freeman's Journal* on 11 December 1882:

> Sir, I beg to state through the columns of your influential journal that my husband, Myles Joyce, now a convict in Galway jail, is not guilty of the crime.
>
> Does not everyone easily imagine a man going before his Almighty God will tell the thruth [*sic*], in telling the thruth they must confess that he never shared in it.
>
> I earnestly beg and implore his Excellency the Lord Lieutenant to examine and consider this hard case of an innocent man, which leaves a widow and five orphans to be before long a dhrift [*sic*] in the world.

She signed off as 'the wife of Myles Joyce that is to be executed on the 15th inst'.

A response to prison governor George Mason from the viceroy, Lord Spencer, coldly stated that the 'Law must take its course'. Five days later, despite Brighid having given birth to a daughter, the executions went ahead.

The *Irish Times* was at the Galway scaffold. The paper's correspondent noted that 'At a quarter-past eight o'clock the prison doors were thrown open':

> With startled looks they marked the wild, hollow eyes, sunken cheeks, and shrunken forms of each other, but not a word passed between them. Myles Joyce came first, between two warders, bareheaded, repeating in Irish the responses to the prayers which were being read by the Revd Mr Grevan. Then came Pat Casey, pinioned, silent, and with a look of great agony on his features. Last appeared Pat Joyce, taller than the others, wearing his hat, silent, too, and walking with firm and steady step …

The executioner, William Marwood, then placed them with the tallest man in the centre and began pinioning the knees. Myles Joyce continued to speak in an 'excited way'. According to the correspondent:

It was impossible to gather the meaning of much that fell from him, even by Irish-speaking persons who were present; but the following sentences have been interpreted for me by one who understands and speaks the language thoroughly, and who was close enough to hear the greater part of what he said. These sentences were: 'I am going before my God. I was not there at all. I had no hand or part in it. I am as innocent as a child in the cradle. It is a poor thing to take this life away on a stage; but I have my priest with me.'

Eight men were convicted on the basis of what emerged later to be perjured evidence. Three of the eight were executed and five imprisoned.

Some time ago, while perusing the British archives in Kew, a reporter, Seán Ó Cuirreáin, discovered that a move to pay the witnesses bore the personal hand of the Lord Lieutenant, Earl Spencer, great-granduncle of the current princes William and Harry. Not only did he compensate three men who claimed to be eyewitnesses, but he paid them well over the going rate: a sum totalling £1,250 (equivalent to about €157,000 today).

The Spenser family offered financial compensation by way of reparation to the descendants of Myles Joyce. Charles Stewart Parnell, leader of the Irish Parliamentary Party, withdrew his support from the Prime Minister, William Gladstone, and the Liberal government when the latter refused to open an inquiry sometime after the executions had been carried out. This precipitated a general election which the Liberals lost.

George Bolton also undertook the investigation into the murder of Thomas Higgins, a caretaker on Lord Ardilaun's estate. This occurred on the road between Clonbur and Cong. Once again, Bolton complained about the number of witnesses who, when called to give evidence in court, feigned memory loss or gave self-contradictory evidence. At the end of a long and complicated trial, the jury found the accused pair guilty of manslaughter.

Without doubt, those were tense times in South Mayo.

44

GEORGE MCNAMARA

George McNamara was surely one of the most colourful characters to ever adorn the pages of history, or at least the history of County Mayo. Stories of George and his lifestyle have been passed down through the centuries from one generation to the next in the manner of the oral tradition.

The common people in Irish society, which had very high illiteracy levels, passed their culture and lore onto the next generation in line by storytelling or some other medium, such as dance or musical airs. Not that the common folk in George McNamara's time had many musical instruments!

People in these days had prodigious memories and that is understandable as there were no other way of information storage or retrieval. The need to commit long tracts of information to memory is no longer a necessity and people of the present day can store and retrieve information in very many ways.

It can be taken for granted that any story passed down in this way is an exact rendition of the original one. Such was the way of the oral tradition: word perfect and every nuance intact since the beginning. The *seanchaí* was a professional storyteller, who might not have been paid for his labours but was a very highly respected member of all communities where few, if any, literate people resided.

Stories about George and other colourful characters were composed by a *seanchaí* and passed down over the years, right on to recent times.

Whatever the merits of the accounts of McNamara's activities that survived through the centuries until now, they are exact copies of what the original composer saw fit to compose.

In simple terms, one could be forgiven for thinking that there were, in fact, two men named George McNamara, a nice one and a nasty one. Stories abound about both and there is really very little common ground when one goes about researching the life and times of this extraordinary character. We know that McNamara was a Clare native, born in 1690. This time of intense religious persecution was known as the Penal Days. A series of laws were enacted (in 1695) to force Irish Roman Catholics and Protestant dissenters (such as Presbyterians) to accept the status of the 'established' or state-supported Anglican Church.

As George was growing up, harsh Penal Laws were enforced, known as the 'Popery Code': Catholics were prohibited from buying land or owning property (such as horses) valued at more than £5. They could no longer stand for elected office or enter the forces or the law. Further penal measures were added in the early years of the eighteenth century. These laws – passed by the ruling Protestants classes in Ireland – were designed to strip the 'backward' Catholic population and dissenters of remaining land, positions of influence and civil rights.

As he was brought up as a Roman Catholic and thus could not become a landowner, George persuaded his brother-in-law, who was a Protestant, to buy an estate in the grounds of Cong Abbey for him. The remains of his mansion there can still be seen in the grounds behind the abbey. (The Irish Tourist Association file records that Bishop Pococke described the Abbey House in 1770 as the most delightfully situated residence he had seen in the course of his travels. Richard Pococke was an English prelate and anthropologist. He was the Bishop of Ossory and Meath, both dioceses of the Church of Ireland. However, he is best known for his travel writings and diaries.)

So, in spite of his Catholic faith, George prospered and the authorities turned a blind eye to the fact that he was clearly breaching the 'Popery Code' by residing in such fine premises. To add to the mystery surrounding his undoubted wealth, he lived an opulent lifestyle, even though he was forbidden by the same code to own or lease land.

If stories about the 'nice' George are to be believed, he was known as 'The Robin Hood of Cong', a fearless character who robbed the rich to aid the poor. Along with two allies and his favourite horse, Venus, George McNamara was involved in various activities in the Cong region, taking goods from the rich and greedy landlords and donating the same to the poor of the neighbouring villages. Many stories are recorded about this gallant man with a social conscience and a wish to support victims of landlordism and suppression at the beginning of the eighteenth century.

George McNamara was described as being a strong, agile and handsome man. He was a superb sportsman, well known for his horsemanship, and was also reputed to be an excellent marksman. He was enraged by the ill treatment of the peasant class and it is said that he settled in Cong with the intention of making life better for the poor of the village. He could see that there was no way in which the tenant farmers could improve their lifestyles or conditions for their families, for if they made an improvement on their leased landholding this encouraged the landlord to levy more taxes. Eviction was the greatest fear of these tenants, and McNamara endeavoured to use his skills and local knowledge to 'disown' some of the irresponsible and cruel landlords and make the poor tenants the benefactors.

According to many accounts, McNamara went to extraordinary lengths to carry out his mission to distribute wealth in the area by taking from the rich and giving to the poor. It appears that he was in the habit of throwing extravagant house parties to which members of the ruling classes were invited. At such events, George appeared to drink heavily and had to excuse himself as his attendants carried him upstairs to his bedchamber. He would arise late in the morning after such a display of inebriation and apologise to all and sundry, promising that he would never make such a show of himself again.

Of course, his guests were anxious to assure him each time that they were not in the least offended by his actions and to put the matter behind him. However, they might not have been so gracious if they had known what his motives for appearing to be drunk were.

Once upstairs and out of sight of his unsuspecting guests downstairs, he would don black clothing and a mask and slip quietly out of the house through a secret passageway and saddle up his beloved horse, Venus. Venus was both sure-footed and fleet-footed and McNamara was able to reach the houses of some of his unsuspecting guests, relieve them of valuables that weren't locked up, and get back to his own home long before daylight.

He managed to avoid arrest because he was quick-witted and enjoyed local support. The authorities may have been suspicious, but nobody could prove that he was the burglar who practised his calling with impunity over many years.

According to tradition, his kitchens were always stocked with foods, which he generously shared with his neighbours. He had a brewery, a fishery, and also ran a farm, so that he could supply various foods to those in need.

He lies buried in the grounds of Cong Abbey.

So much for the legends that grew up around the 'nice' George McNamara – there are just as many about the 'nasty' George!

According to his detractors, he lived a life of debauchery and self-gratification, never allowing anything or anyone to stand in his way. McNamara was involved in litigation over the ownership of the abbey lands in the 1730s. The land and the livestock on it were the property of a rich, young widow who lived abroad and he was charged with stealing and disposing of her property in her absence.

She returned home for the trial and attended the opening session of the court. She was determined to see him punished for his attempt to rob her and revenge was on her mind as the proceedings began. Things looked decidedly bleak for George as the prosecutor listed every wrongdoing and illegal act he had committed over the years. His illegal and immoral activities appeared to be coming to an end as the opposing counsel laid his past career bare with merciless precision.

Then, unbelievably, George was spared the fate he thoroughly deserved when the widow was smitten by his handsome appearance and his magnificent disposition. She decided, there and then, to halt proceedings and had all charges against him dropped. She ignored the counsel of those who knew him well and married him after a brief courtship.

She had a young son who attended school on the Continent and her new husband persuaded her to bring the youngster home so that he could teach him how to manage the property. The poor woman was tricked into doing so and a short while afterwards the boy was found dead on the roadside with his horse grazing nearby. A most tragic incident everyone agreed, as the horse must have been startled and thrown his young rider to his death. There were some who thought otherwise, but felt it prudent to keep their mouths shut and keep their suspicions to themselves.

In her inconsolable grief, his young wife was incapable of managing her property and passed control of her estate over to him. He wasted no time in reverting to his old pleasure-seeking ways. Some months later, the poor woman was found dead, the victim of a stroke or something similar as she lay sleeping. Once more tongues began to wag, but no one was prepared to voice his suspicions. All who knew George was wary of his ungovernable temper. Eventually he spent all of his wife's money and returned to a life of crime. Once again, he struck fear into the hearts of everyone who lived in Cong and the countryside around it.

From this point onwards, stories about George take on a supernatural tint. He was gifted with powers far beyond anything enjoyed by ordinary mortals.

His horse, Venus, or Feenish in some accounts, was said to be able to mount stairs and climb in through windows. This wondrous mare could outrun any other steed alive and could clear 30-feet-wide ravines in full flight from the law.

Rumours began to spread amongst the common people that both McNamara and his horse had acquired magical powers through some underhand means and this, of course, added to their terror of him. But all good things must come to an end and George and his faithful Venus came to the end of their respective careers when they were almost trapped in a bog by a horde of angry victims of his misdeeds.

Horse and rider were lucky to make their way through this morass and leave their pursuers behind them, but poor Venus was unable to go any further and dropped dead at McNamara's feet.

While he thought very little of his wife and others around him, McNamara was inconsolable over the death of his faithful horse and ended his life of hedonism and crime after that. It was said that he lost all of his magic powers when Venus dropped dead and his life fell to pieces afterwards. It is widely assumed that he died a broken man and was buried in the grounds of Cong Abbey.

ABOUT THE AUTHOR

EAMONN HENRY, a retired teacher and native of Swinford, Mayo, has written a wide variety of Mayo-related articles for online publication and has edited the magazine section of mayo-ireland.ie, the most popular and comprehensive website in Connacht. He also runs mayogodhelpus.com and is the author of *The Little Book of Mayo* and *Tales from the West of Ireland*.